YOGA FOR LAWYERS

MIND-BODY TECHNIQUES TO FEEL BETTER ALL THE TIME

HALLIE N. LOVE AND NATHALIE MARTIN

Cover design by Jill Tedhams/ABA Publishing. Interior photographs by Carolyn Wright, The Photography Studio, Santa Fe, New Mexico, www.thephotostudio.com.

Printed in the United States of America.

17 16 15 14   5 4 3 2 1

Library of Congress Cataloging-in-Publication Data
Love, Hallie N. (Hallie N.), author.
  Yoga for lawyers : mind-body techniques to feel better all the time / Hallie N. Love and Nathalie Martin.
    p. cm.
  Includes bibliographical references.

ISBN 978-1-62722-523-6

1. Lawyers—Life skills guides. 2. Lawyers—United States. 3. Yoga. 4. Mind and body—United States. 5. Exercise therapy—United States. 6. Holistic medicine—United States. I. Martin, Nathalie, 1961- author. II. Title.

KF310.A43L68 2014

613.7'046—dc23   2014008280

Discounts are available for books ordered in bulk. Special consideration is given to state bars, CLE programs, and other bar-related organizations. Inquire at Book Publishing, ABA Publishing, American Bar Association, 321 N. Clark Street, Chicago, Illinois 60654-7598.

www.ShopABA.org

With appreciation to all my students throughout the years, and for the well-being of generations to come.
Also to my son, Tristan, with admiration and love.
—Hallie N. Love

❋ ❋

To Steven Keeva, who paved the way for this book and who passed away just as we were starting to write it.
And to my mother JoAnn Martin, who is still a yoga role model and a yogi at 78.
—Nathalie Martin

Table of Contents

Preface

Congratulations on picking up this introduction to mind-body connections for lawyers, and for taking a step toward improving your state of mind, your health, and your practice. We are both attorneys and know how stiff lawyers can become from working long hours. We also know the feeling of brain-fog due to work with no breaks. Finally, since we've been there, we know how busy you are and how precious your time is. In this short book, we can help you become a better lawyer, accomplish more in less time, improve your work-life balance, and feel healthier.

Both of us have worked in large law firms and have experienced burning the candle at both ends. We have dealt with other people's problems, persistent conflict, and the myriad stresses encountered in the practice of law. We have written this book in order to share some simple things you can do throughout your day to improve your state of mind and reinvigorate your body.

While the purpose of this book is to help you improve your law practice by improving your ability to concentrate and your overall state of mind, we have both found that these techniques also improve other aspects of our lives, including our personal relationships.

In this book, we do our best to save you time and improve your chances of success by producing this information in lawyer-friendly terms. We hope to help you reach your goals in all aspects of your life. Enjoy your journey and Namaste! ☀

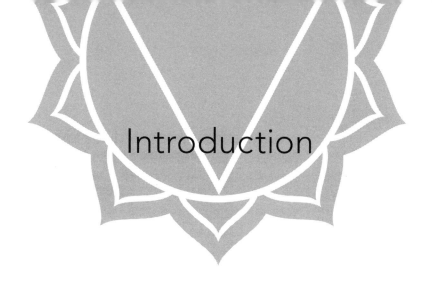

Introduction

Think about how you spend your day. Lawyers are often sedentary beings. We spend most of our days sitting while hunched over on a computer, balancing the phone on one shoulder, and otherwise contorting our bodies while working with words.

This combination of an overworked brain and an inactive body causes the body and the mind to become disconnected and out of balance. Sitting for long hours puts the body into a state of hibernation. Stress weakens our immune systems and exacerbates our already stressful lives. This book provides effective techniques to counterbalance these conditions. We explain techniques to feel better, in simple and clear language.

The ideas we describe here are not complex and you need no experience with yoga or meditation to incorporate them into your life. We describe things you can learn and do easily, some of them in just five minutes at a time. If you do them, you will feel better immediately.

In many ways, this book is different from anything else you can buy. It is written by lawyers for lawyers, and explains things in ways that analytical people like, understand, and embrace. It offers tangible methods and techniques—things you can use in the office, on airplanes, on the phone, in the car, even during a break in a court proceeding or negotiation. We tell you both *how* to use these techniques and *why*, explaining what they can do for you. With practice, anyone from the athletic to the completely out of shape can master these techniques.

We believe the poses and techniques described here can help you:

- experience deep restful sleep;
- relieve nagging or chronic pain in just a few minutes;
- sit and stand better to improve circulation to your vital organs;
- improve brain function through better breathing, posture, and movement;
- improve your ability to practice law by improving productivity and clarity of thinking; and
- improve all aspects of your life, including your practice, by controlling stress and training the mind to focus on more positive thoughts and feelings.

Our goal is to help you incorporate simple methods into your day to connect your mind and your body. This can improve job satisfaction and help create a positive outlook and a better work-life balance. It also may help bring the joie de vivre back into your career and personal life.

Because handling stress well is one of the keys to success as an attorney and also one of the most difficult things to do, we focus on this goal throughout this book. Excessive stress can make us feel foggy and use more energy, both emotional and physical, than is necessary. Our goal is to help you use stress to your advantage and help you function at a higher level, for your own benefit as well as the benefit of your clients, your family and friends, and the legal profession as a whole.

HOW TO USE THIS BOOK

In Chapter 1, we explain why now is the time to learn more about yoga, meditation, and other mindfulness techniques, and use a few testimonials to describe why attorneys, law professors, and judges practice yoga and meditate. In Chapter 2, we briefly explain the science behind stress and the brain. In Chapter 3, we discuss the mind-body connection and why someone would care about such a thing.

Next, in Chapters 4, 5, 6, and 7, we walk you through some postures and techniques you can use for good body alignment and a healthier way to work and move throughout your day. In Chapter 8, we describe various meditation techniques, and in the final chapter, Chapter 9, we discuss mindfulness and lawyering by delving into how yoga and meditation might change your relationship with the legal profession and with the rest of the world.

Use this book as the spirit moves you. There is no need to read it sequentially. Feel free to pick and choose sections based upon your immediate needs. The only thing we really insist upon is that you devise a regular and consistent program for incorporating these techniques into your life and try to stick with it. We wish you the best and hope the experience transforms you. ✳

1

Notes from the Front Line

In this chapter, we briefly explain the mindfulness movement and hear from a few lawyers, judges, and law professors who have used yoga and meditation techniques to improve their work performance and enhance their well-being.

WHY LEARN ABOUT YOGA AND MEDITATION NOW?

As the father of the modern mindfulness movement, Jon Kabat-Zinn, notes in his book *Full Catastrophe Living*, the world has changed incredibly in the past 20 years, perhaps more so than in any 20 year period in history.[1] Laptops, cell phones, the entire digital revolution, all make it possible to be in touch with everyone at all times, 24/7.

The idea of being present in any one moment, though, seems impossible to imagine. Yet, if you are not present, where are you? As Kabat-Zinn notes, life is full of moments and nothing else.[2] One moment, then another moment, and another. What a luxury to savor each as they come up, even some of the time. We can choose to dwell on the past or dream about the future all or most of the time, but if we do so, we miss life as it actually happens.

The pressure to always be somewhere other than the here-and-now, along with the stress of adapting to all of life's stimuli, is starting to take a toll on us, collectively and individually. Indeed, we are starting to lose the ability to concentrate even when we know it is critically important to pay attention to the here-and-now.

As Professors Lisle Baker and Daniel P. Brown recount in their law review article about the lost art of paying attention, Democratic New York State Senate Majority Leader Malcolm Smith lost his senate seat, in large part, because he fiddled with his Black-Berry while meeting with billionaire Thomas Golisano. Golisano, an independent, had made a special trip to Albany to meet with Smith to discuss important law reform. Golisano was so annoyed by Smith's lack of present-moment attention that he "went to the Republicans and told them he'd be happy to unseat Smith, perhaps in the hopes of having him replaced with someone who could pay attention for a few minutes."[3] As this story shows, being able to be present is important to our clients and our professional success.

LAWYERING AND UNIQUE STRESS

Like many professions, lawyering is getting harder and more complex. Stress, information overload, and losing the ability to pay attention are present for all of society but as lawyers we have special circumstances that make it even more important to be present. Lawyers deal with other people and other people's problems all day. We need to be able to listen to them in order to actually serve them.

Moreover, we often lack control over our everyday lives and frequently find it impossible to please everyone, no matter what we do. We worry about money and billable hours, and work very long hours. The economy is particularly volatile for many people right now and most lawyers are feeling it.

Even in more prosperous economic times, stress-related problems among law students and lawyers are well-documented; lawyers rank among the highest in professions marred by depression, anxiety, stress, substance abuse, and suicide.[4] These problems create a cloud over our profession.

We also sit at a desk all day, typically moving very little and living most of our lives from the neck up. Many of us have very little awareness of our bodies and think of our bodies as wholly separate from our most useful organ, the brain. In reality, the mind and body are connected and what we think about can deeply influence both our physical and our mental health.

Moreover, a poorly maintained body can also influence our ability to think and work clearly. As Kabat-Zinn explains:

bodies are subject to inevitable breakdown. But they do seem to break down sooner and to heal less rapidly and

less completely if they are not cared for and listened to in some basic ways. For this reason, taking proper care of your body is of great importance in both the prevention of disease and the work of healing from illness, disease, or injury.[5]

Kabat-Zinn also notes that bodies that are not in motion can suffer from disuse atrophy, which weakens immunity and makes us more likely to become sick.[6] Fortunately, even small changes in how we move, hold our bodies, and occupy our minds, can create drastic improvements in our physical and mental health.

The purpose of this short book is to show you some accessible methods for tapping into these techniques. From our own experience, and the experiences of many people with whom we have worked, these techniques improve well-being almost immediately, and with sustained regular practice, can transform your entire life. The benefits are both physical and mental.

While not every lawyer is concerned with physical fitness, we can't think of a single one that doesn't care about clear thinking and maximum mental health. We hope this book will help you maximize these and other skills.

STORIES FROM THE LEGAL COMMUNITY ON THE BENEFITS OF YOGA AND MEDITATION

Integrative attorney Stu Webb, the founder and Godfather of collaborative law, reports that meditation quiets his mind and allows him to be present in the NOW, free of the distractions that come from busy mental activity. This in turn improves his legal practice by allowing him to focus on what is most important to the people involved. Phoenix integrative attorney Pamela J.P. Donison adds that:

Meditation and yoga help me tap into my own inner wisdom and empower me to hold compassion and empathy in even the most conflicted situations. As a family law attorney, mediator, and peacemaker, my first priority is to bring my best self to the room. While I practice yoga a few times a month, I meditate *every* day and have found it to be essential to my ability to work with people in transition. I "refresh" that practice before each client interaction by spending just a few minutes centering, breathing, and setting an intention for the meeting. This small ritual has a powerful effect on both me and my clients—I come to them in a calm, aware, and mindful state which sets the stage for a mirror neuron interplay that allows the client to also become more calm and mindful. I believe everyone benefits from meditation, but it is *essential* for attorneys to maintain our health and well-being in a stressful, adversarial, and competitive field.

Similarly, Washington state attorney Cat J. Zavis has found that:

through my regular meditation practice I am able to draw on the practice in the midst of a collaborative meeting. I can ground myself and remind myself to tap into compassion, open-heartedness, to notice my own emotions and make sure they are not driving my interactions. I remember to be a witness to what is happening rather than being swept up in the upsets and stresses that the clients are experiencing.

From a law professor:

I first started practicing yoga in 1999, when I was a new law professor and was working in our live-client clinical law program. Before becoming a law professor, I led a stressful life as a big firm lawyer, married to another big firm lawyer. My mother bought me a yoga kit comprised of a DVD, a mat, a strap, and a block. From here I bought more DVDs and finally began attending beginner classes at gyms and studios. I am still a beginner and am happy that yoga is the one aspect of my life that is not competitive.

What drew me to yoga and kept me practicing was the way it improved my sleep. Right away. And I noticed it every time I did yoga, even years after I began. While I suppose it is less stressful than working in a large, big city law firm, clinical teaching made me very nervous and full of stress. It was new, I was trying to balance long teaching hours with plenty of publication to grease the promotion and tenure wheels. I was seeing extremely needy people and the inadequacies of the law for the first time. I was supposed to let my students lawyer the cases when they really didn't know how. Yoga made me feel better. It helped me let go of things that I simply had no control over.

I still lead a crazy life, far more scheduled than need be. But yoga is with me, by my side. It helps me be a better lawyer, teacher, mentor, and hopefully, person. I am not perfect, but life is so much better for me and for those around me with these newfound tools.

From a non-profit lawyer who works with battered women:

For over twelve years, I have worked at a non-profit providing legal representation to immigrant survivors of domestic and sexual violence, which is deeply stressful. For me, selfcare prominently includes yoga and meditation. If my mind is inundated with tragedy all the time, it can't function as well either personally or professionally. If I am completely focused on my breathing and my body's alignment, my brain cannot also be fixated on whether my clients are safe or if I am doing enough to help them. If I am occupied by noticing the connection between my exhalations and going just a *little* deeper into a pose, my mind isn't thinking about blood, bruises, tears, or suffering. If I am envisioning the blood flowing to every part of my body or concentrating on a focal point in the center of my skull, it's a lot harder to dedicate as much energy to thinking about the endless ways people seem to get hurt.

The impacts of yoga and meditation for me are not just felt "on the mat," as they say. At work when I am faced with the intense emotions of sorrow and despair, I can notice my breath and what my muscles feel like. I can feel more patience towards my clients and others with whom I interact professionally if I have cultivated more patience towards myself by practicing yoga and meditation. I'm not saying it's automatic, or that there is no pain or frustration, but without the skills I have learned from practicing yoga and meditation, I would have burned out a long time ago.

From another non-profit attorney who works for children's rights:

I love being a lawyer. I thought that my love of lawyering would insulate me from all those stories of folks that burn out because their lives are out of balance. Almost every day for the last twenty years I have been blessed to work with families and children, trying to find the best way to leverage support to ensure that children are loved, educated, and safe. I would get up every morning and work, help my kids get off to school, work, help my kids with dinner, discussing thoughts about their day, preparing for the next day, connect with my husband and then work again. My life was incredibly rich. I met wonderful folks, my kids grew up and my husband still has my back in life.

I wasn't insulated. I hit a wall. Hard. Was it too many years bearing witness to people struggling with poverty, abuse, lack of resources? Too little time finding ease and tenderness in life? I am sure I don't know what all the lessons to be learned from this year are yet. But I do know that yoga was my raft in the storm. Because I am new to yoga, I have had to start at the beginning. This means I have had to consciously be willing to learn, fall, get up, keep going. Some days I can't seem to focus or bend or balance and other days my practice seems almost effortless and I land new poses or stretch to new lengths. And what I do on my mat doesn't really matter to anyone else in the room.

Yoga, for me, has been an antidote to the perfectionism that our profession breeds, which at its best is a laudable aspiration and, at the extreme, is untenable. So how has yoga changed my practice as a lawyer? First and foremost, I leave the office to go to yoga before I go home. This means I leave the office before 6 nearly every evening. It also means that when I do get home, I am more open and present to my family. The really surprising aspect of all of this to me is that not only have my personal relationships been enriched, but my professional relationships have also benefited. I am not sure how to best articulate it but somehow I have shifted my focus, just a bit, finding new ways to be present, to listen, and to appreciate the process of relating to people, regardless of the outcome or product (which is no less important than ever).

We all need ports in the storm of life and practicing yoga is a chance to find my own port each time I unroll my mat.

From author Hallie Love:

I entered law school and my first years of legal practice brimming with enthusiasm and idealism for the noble profession of law. Through the years, though, the "normal" stressors of legal practice—relentless demands, impossible caseloads, and stressed out bosses, to name a few—became insurmountable for me. I exited law in a frazzled state. It was yoga that revived me. It was then that I decided to shift gears. For over a decade I have focused on teaching lawyers and other professionals the profound well-being to be gained through yoga therapy, Yoga Nidra meditation, and positive psychology. Lawyers have continually informed me of the value they have received from mind-body training. Here's what a few are saying:

"…my productivity at work has skyrocketed…my state of mind is balanced…I'm much more at peace for the rest of the day…"

"The legal profession is challenging and stressful. To be a "well attorney" requires more than average stress management. Yoga is a powerful tool for attorneys."

"Prior meditation classes have felt like failures. The Yoga Nidra practice worked for me, and I felt alert and invigorated afterwards."

"I was making myself sick with stress…After Yoga Nidra I felt much calmer and 200 percent physically better. No more migraines…now able to listen patiently to others. I feel more positive, less burdened, and the hard things in my life go a whole lot easier. I sleep better, too."

This book is a solid foundation for anyone. We offer it in gratitude for all the benefits that we and others have received from yoga.

YOGA CLASSES

Today, over 20 million people practice yoga. Many people's first exposure to yoga is through DVDs and books, or perhaps classes at a gym. This is in part because many people are intimidated by yoga studios. They feel unsure of what they will encounter if they enter a yoga studio, and some have even had a bad experience or two. Perhaps they were admonished in a class for leaving to use the restroom or drinking water during class, so they decided not to return.

If you do decide to venture into a yoga class and you are new, pick a class for beginners and try to get there a bit early to talk to the teacher. Tell the teacher it is your first time and that you may need to get up now and then, or tell the teacher about any injuries or issues you have. Sit in the back. Try a few different teachers until you find one you are comfortable with. You should look forward to attending the class and relate to the teacher as a person, as well as a yoga instructor. ❋

2

Stressed Out

Stress is a part of every attorney's life, as well as the lives of many other people in American society. There is no way to completely avoid stress and some of it is even good for us, as it helps us perform at our peak. When stress becomes chronic, it hurts more than it helps.

Some lawyers wear stress like a badge. As attorneys, it is common for us to confuse and conflate two very different concepts: on the one hand, fear, worry, tension, anxiety, and exhaustion; on the other, adrenaline, invigorating excitement to do something amazing, to do one's best, to be completely ready and to bring it on! We tend to think we need the worry, tension, and anxiety to do well, when what we are really looking for is those latter experiences, without the worry and tension. We think it is fabulous to be excited and full of adrenaline, but less than fabulous to be genuinely freaked out.

The most common risks of stress relate directly to the practice of law, and these effects are well-documented in medical literature. Too much stress literally ages our bodies and brains[7] and impairs our ability to make good decisions.[8] Stress can impair lawyers' capacities to excel in the practice of law, including the ability to uphold the Code of Ethics and the Creed of Professionalism. Cases from disciplinary boards around the country are replete with examples of lawyers who have breached professional obligations to clients and committed malpractice because they handled stress poorly and self-medicated with drugs and alcohol.[9]

Decades of empirical studies at institutions like Harvard and Yale document and measure the many ways in which continuous and pervasive stress impairs cognitive function. All reach the same conclusion: People under severe stress can't think straight, and often, judgment is impaired.

Experiments on students show that high stress levels result in lower grades.[10] Further studies show that anxious people are more likely to rely on the advice of others and less on their own judgment, are less able to discern good versus bad decisions, and are less able to spot conflicts of interest.[11] The bottom line? Sure, some stress can amp you up for a big brief, court appearance, or meeting, but too much can cloud your judgment and thinking.

WHAT STRESS?

There is a lot of stress in most people's lives, not just lawyers. No doubt though, lawyers experience much more stress than most people.[12] What are the most stressful things lawyers do? Start a journal and make your own list. You need to know your own trigger points in order to counter these negative effects. Here are some common ones:

- Too many billable hours
- Too much debt—student loans, mortgage, credit cards, car payments, etc.
- Difficult conversations
- Negative people
- Conflicts in personal life
- Telling people no
- Public speaking
- Thorny problems that seem to have no solution
- Criticism
- Attempting to internalize and correct for criticism
- Overscheduling
- Multitasking
- Boring, thankless tasks
- Lack of control over life or schedule
- Too little time

THE SCIENCE BEHIND STRESS

How can we gain relief or at least awareness of the difficulties stress causes in our bodies? In part by becoming aware of the scientific data behind stress. Chronic stress causes what scientists call a chronic stress response. By becoming aware of stress, we can turn it off when we need to.[13]

THE PRIMITIVE BRAIN AND THE THINKING BRAIN: WE CAN'T USE BOTH AT THE SAME TIME

All humans have two brains. Both are anatomically separate, and each has a different purpose. Often the two unique purposes are at odds with one another, dueling for dominance. One is the oldest, or primitive, brain. The other brain is the rational, or thinking, brain.

THE PRIMITIVE BRAIN

The primitive brain runs our bodies, our metabolism, our emotions, and the stress response. Evolutionarily speaking, its design goes back to our most primitive past. As discussed in more detail in the next chapter, the primitive brain was very helpful to us in the past, when only the fittest survived. It is the control center for fear and aggression (the fight or flight response), our deepest and most primitive emotions. The primitive brain is based in the amygdala. The fight or flight response is triggered by the amygdala, a small almond-shaped region in the midbrain's limbic region below the cortex.

Thousands of years ago, the fight or flight response was necessary for survival. During this time, humans did not have to think logically. In danger, the amygdala sounded the alarm, prompting activation of the sympathetic nervous system, which flooded adrenaline, noradrenaline, and cortisol into the blood. The physiological responses to those stress hormones provide everything one needs to fight to the death, freeze so no one sees you, or run like crazy. In this condition, all your energy is dedicated to survival. The stress chemicals increase your physical strength, narrow your vision so you can zero in on the threat, increase your heart rate, contract your muscles, and route your blood from your brain into your trunk. The primitive brain senses a threat and simply reacts.

The primitive brain does not distinguish between physical and psychological threats. Every type of stressor releases a torrent of stress hormones. In law practice, this torrent is so commonplace it may seem "normal." A deadline, a disappointment, an angry boss, a conflict with a colleague or client, an imposing workload, an unreturned phone call—all these threats can move us into fear or aggression instinctively.

Fear and aggression take many forms. Some common forms include frustration, irritability, impatience, insecurity, anxiety, anger, blame, or resentment. These emotions limit our thought to a narrow view that obscures creative solutions. In fight mode, we turn our negative emotions against other people; in flight mode, we turn our negative emotions on ourselves.

Not only do negative emotions drain energy, interfere with clear thinking, and make us less effective, they also have a strong impact on others. The research is clear—negative emotions are contagious.

Because all energy goes to prepare the body to fight or flee during times of stress, all nonessential functions of the body shut down. The digestive system and kidneys shut down; the liver stops cleaning blood; the immune system stops activating; the brain abandons long term thinking and development of long term memory; tissue repair stops; every scrap of energy swings from long term to immediate survival.

THE THINKING BRAIN

Through evolution we developed the other brain, the thinking brain. We use this brain to think logically, draw conclusions from many pieces of information, and plan for the future. The thinking brain's purpose reflects a huge evolutionary leap—think then react. Most of a lawyer's daily work is much better served by this brain.

The big problem is that the thinking brain shuts down when the stress response turns on. This is nature's survival design because conscious thinking slows down the speed of reacting to life-threatening situations. It takes the thinking brain two full seconds to register and respond to imminent danger, whereas the primitive brain reacts in two 100ths of a second.

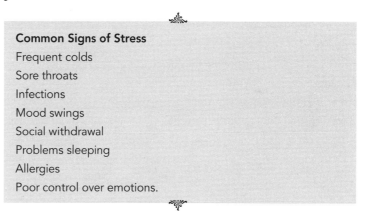

Common Signs of Stress
Frequent colds
Sore throats
Infections
Mood swings
Social withdrawal
Problems sleeping
Allergies
Poor control over emotions.

Cortisol and the Adrenal Glands

To explain a bit more about the anatomy, the brain's emotional control system is found in the limbic system, which regulates fear, anger, pleasure, and sadness, as well as stress. If you sense a direct threat, your autonomic nervous system activates a complex process designed to keep you safe, a process that involves hormones, the adrenal glands, and the bloodstream.

In stressful situations, the adrenal glands (located on top of your kidneys) release a chemical called cortisol, which the blood carries to the brain. Cortisol is the agent that tells your body that danger is imminent, and you are either going to have to fight or flee—the fight or flight response we discuss above.

Hormones are responsible for activating your adrenal glands, but also for triggering the physiological processes for calming or relaxing your body, or returning it to homeostasis or equilibrium.

In fact, during excessive or extensive stress, cortisol gathers and stays in the hippocampus (the little seahorse-shaped structure) which is the part of the brain in charge of memory and learning. All that cortisol in the hippocampus makes it hard to think straight. This is why individuals in the course of trauma or high stress situations report being confused and unable to think clearly. The hippocampus literally atrophies under excessive and prolonged stress.[14] Indeed, large amounts of cortisol impede the ability to draw on long-term memory and to think clearly. What's worse, cortisol has been shown to damage and kill brain cells in the hippocampus, and as a result, cause premature brain aging. We will refer back to these psychological conditions throughout the various chapters of this book.

OTHER HORMONES AND THE ADRENAL GLANDS: WHY OUR WAISTS AND MEDICAL BILLS ARE GROWING

The adrenal glands also release hormones such as adrenaline that increase heart rate, blood pressure, and breathing. They also dump excess glucose and fatty acids into the blood. Again, if this is a constant mental state, the cardiovascular system is strained and the immune system is suppressed. This condition destroys memory cells, causes fat deposits to accumulate at the waist rather than in the hips and buttocks, and puts us at risk of heart disease, cancer, obesity, and diabetes.

STRESS AND MULTITASKING

Lawyers love multitasking. We are taught to juggle many things at once, but this is not necessarily good for the brain or for the tasks at hand.[15] We've all noticed examples of this. If you are constantly thinking of ten things at once, your brain is not operating at its best. The result is chronic exhaustion and mental lethargy, which overtaxes those adrenal glands again. When a person's adrenal glands are overtaxed with no prolonged periods of calm in between, brain function is compromised. Conversely, learning positive ways to manage your stress can improve your health dramatically.

HOW CONTEMPLATIVE PRACTICES LIKE YOGA AND MEDITATION HELP WITH STRESS

As discussed above, sustained stress has a deleterious impact upon us, with studies showing that stress leads to more rapid memory loss and impairs our ability to make good decisions.[16] Stress also ages the brain.[17]

Conversely, study after study confirms that contemplative practices like yoga and meditation enhance mental and physical well-being,[19] overall happiness,[20] and cognitive abilities.[21] Meditation (the subject of Chapter 8) and yoga (the subject of much of this book) help relieve stress.[22] Mindfulness meditation and other contemplative practices have a positive influence on the brain and on thinking by decreasing perceived stress, improving concentration, and enhancing one's general sense of well-being.[23] More specifically, Eileen Luders at UCLA's Lab of Neuro Imaging has found that meditation increases gray matter in the brain, creates stronger connections between brain regions, and reduces age-related brain thinning.[24] In 2012, she reported finding mindfulness meditation to be associated with larger amounts of gyrification, the process of creating folds in the cortex. Gyrification is thought to allow the brain to process information faster, which is particularly relevant to the work we do as lawyers.[25] ✳

3

More on the Mind-Body Connection

The last chapter discussed some of the negative consequences of multitasking, or simply neglecting to do things to counterbalance the stress in your life. Some of these consequences relate directly to one's ability to practice law effectively and ethically. Others harm your body in measurable ways, causing heart disease and damaging brain cells.

Research by the father of modern positive psychology, Martin Seligman, shows that attorneys are among the most unhappy people in society, particularly because of three things: they tend to be pessimists, they often have little control over their lives, and they are involved in one big win-lose enterprise, namely the legal system.[26]

No doubt, legal education exacerbates our susceptibility to stress. In law school we learn to look for defects and holes in arguments. We call it "issue spotting" and "learning to think like a lawyer." We train ourselves to be critical thinkers. This process is described aptly by law professor Charles Halpern in his book, *Making Waves and Riding Currents*, in which he described his own law school experience:

> We were learning the language and the tough demeanor
> of lawyer discourse. Our vocabulary became skewed. Being

tough-minded, hard-nosed, and thick-skinned were virtues; there was little talk of altruism or kindness. During a contract negotiation, for example, our job as lawyers was to imagine all the negative outcomes that might possibly happen and draft contract language that would protect our clients' interests in the event of fraud or chicanery by the other contracting parties. The law presented a Darwinian world, and the possibility that people would act out of selfless or generous motives was considered highly unlikely. I found it alarmingly easy to slip into this mindset—suspicious, lawyerly, aggressive.[27]

While we can sometimes further our legal careers with analytical thinking, defensive posturing, and looking for and zeroing in on weaknesses in opposing counsel, there is a sizeable downside to these habits. By training and thinking this way hour after hour, we ingrain neural pathways in our brains that look for and target the negative. This "legal thinking" can lead to a fault-finding, energy-draining, hypercritical, overly suspicious, and stress-producing mindset. It can also lead to a focus on negativity and cynicism and for some, depression. The irony is that despite all this negative training, positive thinking and empathy toward others often produces better results for us and our clients, not to mention our entire social circle.

Here we elaborate a bit further on what we alluded to in Chapter 2, namely that the mind and the body are intimately connected. One necessarily affects the other. We also discuss what you can do about this.

YOU CAN START CHANGING YOUR BRAIN RIGHT NOW

Much of the rest of this book is designed to help you respond to your work and your stress in a helpful and positive way. While many future chapters focus on relieving stress in the body, relieving mental stress is even more important. You can use your mind alone, right now, to change your brain processes for the better.

As Dr. Rick Hanson, a neuropsychologist and author of *Buddha's Brain* explains, one easy way to train your brain is to linger over good experiences and let go of negative experiences more quickly. What we think about can change the neural connections in the brain. Since we are what we think, we can control many of our brain functions which can in turn change the brain forever. As the Buddha himself once said, "whatever one frequently thinks and ponders upon, that will become the inclination of his mind."[29]

THE NEGATIVITY BIAS: KICK IT TO THE CURB

Scientists are very familiar with something called the negativity bias. Because the brain's functions were designed thousands of years ago to protect us from saber-toothed tigers and other real dangers, our ancestors (the people who survived the tigers) were nervous by nature. They focused hard on the things that could hurt them much harder than they focused on the pleasurable aspects of life, so they could live to create us! In other words, by necessity, they were nervous Nellies and Normans. According to Dr. Hanson, we are Velcro for the bad things and Teflon for the good ones. Without some counterbalancing of our natural instincts, bad things stick to us and good things roll right off.

> **Try Dr. Hanson's Technique**
> Right now, to balance out the fact that Mother Nature tilted us toward thinking about bad things, bring to mind something you love or are grateful for, intensify it, and let it sink in for 15 seconds. Practice this every day until this becomes second nature.

We focused on the negative in the past to survive, and stress was a useful attribute for survival back in the day. But back in the day, people were dead by age 30 and the short-term benefits of stress outweighed long-term costs. Now that we live much longer, these negative biases do not serve us. They cause excess wear and tear on our bodies and our brains.

It is an oversimplification to simply tell yourself to "think positively" and deny all of the negative events that happen in life. Tons of annoying and downright life-shattering things happen to us all, but with all the genetics working toward getting us to focus on those terrible things, we need to work on putting more emphasis on the positive and beautiful, in order to balance it all out and give the good a fighting chance.

Dr. Hanson suggests that to counterbalance the brain's historic focus on the negative, we need to put special effort into actively focusing on the positive. To balance out the negativity that we store and recycle over and over again, Hanson suggests we consciously take in and store the good. He suggests we savor positive experiences and thoughts for 10–20 seconds so these good experiences become habit. If we intensify these thoughts, Hanson claims, it will prime the memory system in a lasting way and cause positive changes in the brain.

Similarly, we often pay way too much attention to our own failures and not enough attention to our successes. Positive psychologist Barbara Fredrickson found that in general, each negative feeling is three times as powerful as a positive one.[30] In other words, it generally takes three times as many positive experiences for most of us to overcome one negative one. The first step to overcoming this tendency is to become aware of the tendency and the second is to become mindful of your body and the way you experience emotions physically. You can then use this experience to scan the body, breathe into the areas in which you experience the negative feelings (more on this in Chapter 8), and use your own mind to counterbalance these negative experiences and emotions and focus more on the positive ones.

BRAIN WAVES AND YOUR RELATIONSHIPS WITH OTHERS

These positive thought principles apply to our relationships with others as well. As author Chade-Meng Tan explains in his book *Search Inside Yourself*:

[We] think what we become. The method is itself simple: invite a thought to arise in your mind often enough and it will become a mental habit. For example, if every time you see another person you wish for that person to be happy, then eventually, it will become your mental habit and whenever you meet another person, your instinctive first thought is to wish for that person to be happy. After a while you develop an instinct for kindness. You become a kind person. Your kindness shows in your face, posture, and attitude every time you meet somebody. People will become attracted to your personality, not just your good looks.[31]

Jokes aside, this quote contains two important truths: first, you can control what you decide to think about and second, developing a knack for kindness will improve your success at work, not to mention your personal life.

Additionally, it can help to focus on the feelings and views of others rather than ourselves when things go wrong. When we feel hurt or misunderstood, our thoughts are dominated by how awful the other person is, all because we want to avoid feeling that hurt. If we can bring conscious awareness to this tendency, we can tame the ruminations and obsessive thoughts.[32] We can also improve our interpersonal relationships.

In sum, how and what we think about also creates visible, physical changes in our brain cells. Studies of long-time meditators (the subject of Chapter 8) show that meditation increases the thickness in the regions of the brain associated with attention and processing sensory input, improving concentration.[33] This means that by learning to control our own thoughts, we can change our brain for the better rather than letting the environment, other people, our difficult cases and clients, or any of life's many challenges, negatively influence us.

MUSIC AND BRAIN ACTIVITY

Studies show that music can do a brain a world of good. For example, one recent study shows that listening to music improves cognitive recovery following a stroke.[34] Another study shows that listening to music can reduce blood pressure.[35] Listening to music with calm, full attention can even clear the brain the way some meditation might. Just make sure the lyrics are positive and you like the music.

YOGA AND DEPRESSION, PERFORMANCE ANXIETY, AND CREATIVITY

Yoga is a powerful antidote to depression and may have saved some lives as a result.[36] According to scientific studies, yoga releases natural substances in the brain that act as strong antidepressants and can permanently change a person's emotional outlook for the better. In her book *Yoga for Depression*, Amy Weintraub elaborates, noting that even a single yoga class has been scientifically shown to leave psychiatric patients with a sense of relaxation and mild euphoria for several hours.[37]

William Broad, author of *The Science of Yoga*, also cites a study in which beginner musicians with performance anxiety found that regular yoga and meditation practice greatly decreased performance anxiety and improved performance.[38] Broad reports that yoga and meditation also improve creativity, though more study of this topic is needed.[39]

YOGA AND OVERALL HEATH

As if the benefits noted previously were not enough, Broad notes that studies show that regular yoga practice can reduce heart rate and blood pressure, boost immunity, and prevent disease.[40] Indirectly, then, yoga can reduce stroke, cardiovascular disease, and kidney disease. This is big news, as heart disease is currently the number one killer in the industrialized world. Yoga also has been found to reduce cholesterol, improve blood clotting, and raise antioxidant levels. As far as general health is concerned, Chinese studies have found that patients who do yoga have fewer hospital visits, less need for drug therapy, and consistent with other studies, fewer death-inducing heart attacks.

Additionally, yoga wards off aging by making the spine suppler and thus younger. For example, yoga teachers in a Taiwanese study were shown to have less degenerative spine disease. The vagus nerve, which runs all the way from the brainstem to the lungs, heart, stomach, liver, spleen, colon, and abdomen, is stimulated by yoga. This promotes longevity and slows the biological clock. Another study of 50–80 year olds showed that those who did yoga for an hour a day, six days a week, for just three months had significant reductions in cholesterol, blood pressure, and disturbing thoughts. As Broad reports, this study has implications for longevity, tissue renewal, disease prevention, and even increases in life span.[41]

THE IMPORTANCE OF SLEEP

We know it makes no sense to tell you that you need to get more sleep as you are no doubt doing your best. What we will tell you is why sleep is important and what functions sleep serves. While this is a dramatic oversimplification, in basic terms there are two general types of sleep: REM, which is active dreaming sleep used to process emotions and difficult scenarios, and deep sleep, which is used to advance learning and memory. You need both REM and deep sleep to function at your highest and best level.

REM sleep is valuable in helping us process emotions, particularly difficult ones. This may explain why, in the middle of a difficult situation, we feel so much better after a good night's sleep.[42] Sleep actually helps us selectively preserve and enhance positive emotions, and downgrade negative ones. It is during REM sleep that our body produces human growth hormone (HGH), which repairs damage and heals injuries. REM sleep also facilitates protein synthesis and brain cell restoration.

Deep, non-REM sleep helps us remember correct sequencing of events and many other things, as well as how to learn complicated tasks. This is because the brain consolidates information in an organized way during deep sleep. There are several different types of memory. There is declarative memory, which includes retrievable, fact-based information. There is episodic memory, which focuses on events from your life. Finally, there is procedural memory, which allows us to remember how to do something. Researchers have designed ways to test each of them.

In almost every study, no matter which type of memory was involved, one fact remained constant: After first learning something, be it a long, complex, and interrelated web of substantive material, a memorized chart or visual aid, or even a physical skill like skiing or playing tennis, sleeping on it improved performance. It is as if our brains squeeze in some extra practice time while we

are asleep. Some studies show that for every two hours we spend awake, the brain needs an hour of sleep.

In sum, quality sleep is necessary for a healthy body, clear thinking, and rich memory, as well as for processing our waking experiences. Clearly, sleeping plays a crucial role in helping us become better lawyers, and may even help us grasp the meaning in our own lives. Go ahead then. Stop preparing for trial and go to bed.

THE MIND-BODY CONNECTION IN THE OFFICE AND ELSEWHERE

Just being more aware of how you hold and move your body and making appropriate changes can help you feel better immediately. For example, think about the shape of your physical body when you do your work. If you are like most people, you are usually hunched over your computer, shoulders rolled in and forward, arms hanging to the front, and neck cranked forward and down. Alternatively, you are leaning back or to the side in your chair, completely collapsed, abdominal muscles loose with all your other muscles disengaged as well. Perhaps you alternate from one of these positions to another restlessly.

Now sit up straight, raise your head over your shoulders and bring those shoulders down and onto your back. Breathe deeply, as if your life depended on it. Now stand up. A recent public radio show described how certain homeless people in New York slept sitting up on moving trains at night to avoid being rolled or moved on by the police. These people slept hunched over while the trains rattled through the night. As if being homeless were not enough, these poor people have to sleep sitting up. We, on the other hand, can move any time we like. We have almost complete control over what we decide to do with our bodies, to sit, stand, lie down, almost whenever we like. We ought not squander this incredible freedom by remaining seated through most of our lives.

Sitting is one of the worst things you can do to your body. Indeed, recent research even shows that sitting all day can be more harmful to your mind and body than smoking cigarettes.[43] Several new studies show that prolonged sitting is linked to increased risk of heart disease, obesity, diabetes, cancer, and even early death. When you sit for long periods of time, your body goes into storage mode and stops working as effectively as it should. What's worse, the more hours a day you sit, the greater your likelihood of developing one or more of these diseases, just as with smoking.

By necessity, most of us are sitting at a desk, on the phone or on the computer, for ten or more hours a day. Even if you do an hour of cardio exercise a day, it won't make up for all this back-to-back sitting. The body is made up of bones, ligaments, tendons, and fascia. The ligaments and fascia are stiff like credit cards. If you bend them once or twice, they pop back. If you bend them and hold that position more or less constantly, they will permanently crease. This is why stretching and moving the body can permanently increase health.

While most of us have desk jobs, this does not mean we are tied to our desks or our chairs. There are alternatives to sitting while we work. Some lawyers love stand-up desks. Others just make sure they get up and walk around once every hour or so, which has been shown to drastically improve health. Others sit on exercise balls to make sure their cores are engaged. So stand up and walk around, visit a friend, or wash your hands.

Here we provide a bit more detail about how sitting harms us. Frequent sitting deforms the hips and hip flexors and hamstrings, the shoulders and chest, and the neck. In a seated position the hips are flexed, which shortens the hip flexors. Sitting also contorts the hamstring muscles on the backs of your thighs, making it more difficult to move both the hips and knees. The hamstrings are elongated near the hips and shortened at the knee. This is what gives chronic sitters chronically tight hamstrings.

Driving Tips for Sitting up Straighter

Get into your car and sit up nice and straight. Set the rear view mirrors perfectly. As you drive, keep checking that you can still see. If not, you are slouching.

Another good auto tip: If it's comfortable for you, sit with a folded blanket or even a yoga mat under your tailbone. Do what it takes to make sure you are sitting on your sitting bones and not the bottom of your sacrum, even in the car.

Any form of sitting, even with the best posture, will cause the hips, pelvic muscles, and tendons and ligaments to shorten. The postures in Chapters 4, 5, 6, and 7 can help combat these problems. Additionally, backbends can help balance out virtually every daily activity in which we engage.

TIPS FOR FREQUENT SITTERS

1. Get up and walk around at least once every 50–60 minutes. This should be possible at virtually any time, except perhaps in a plane or on a long car ride.
2. When you do sit, make sure your feet reach the floor and your thigh bones (femurs) are parallel to the floor. In other words, your knee joints and hip joints should be at right angles. It is virtually impossible to engage your core when you are seated and your knees are below or above your hips.
3. Sit on your sitting bones, not your sacrum (the bottom of your pelvic bone).
4. Sit in a chair with a back that is shorter than your shoulders, and bend backwards over the back of the chair every 50 minutes or so. This will open your chest and improve breathing.
5. While seated, place a rolled-up yoga mat (or something else like a sweater or suit jacket, anything you have lying around) behind you vertically as you lean back in your chair. Alternatively, use a lumbar support across your low back as you sit.
6. Try not to cross your legs or at least alternate them if you must cross them. Crossing your legs the same way each time stretches out one side of your body and shortens the other, causing pain and poor alignment.
7. Draw the tummy in and melt the shoulders away from your ears and down your back.
8. Sit close to your desk so you do not need to bend forward to reach anything.

MORE DETAIL ON SITTING CORRECTLY

Good posture is simply good body biomechanics from proper alignment. A real problem is that a lot of tight and short muscles or joint soreness and stiffness pull you and torque you and won't let you sit in good alignment. Bad posture pulls your bones and joints out of alignment, including your vertebrae. You end up with nagging pain in your neck, shoulders, hips, and back. Use Rx Yoga at home to stretch muscles in key places in your legs, pelvis, back, and shoulders to make it possible for you to sit in good posture. Sit in good posture and notice how much easier it is to stretch at work and at home. Consistently sit better and notice chronic pains improve. Sitting well also enhances circulation to vital organs and provides more oxygen to your brain.

EXERCISE 1: HOW TO SIT WELL

When you sit, practice aligning your body in 8 easy steps:

1. Feet are flat on the floor, hip-width, and parallel;
2. Knees are 90 degrees over ankles;
3. Back is wide and spine is neutral;
4. Thighs are facing straight up, and hamstrings are facing straight down flat and wide across the backs of the legs;
5. Pelvis remains in neutral position (neither posterior nor anterior tilt). With pelvis in neutral notice how the sitting bones are level with the pubic bone (and not on the front or back edge). Feel how the low belly automatically draws in because of the structural alignment of the neutral pelvis, and not because of any active muscular action; feel how the rib-cage doesn't jut forward or back but simply remains neutral;

6. Spine lifts tall and side waists lengthen increasing the distance between the ribs and the pelvis even as the back and pelvis stay neutral;
7. Shoulders roll so they line up with ears and hips while back and ribs remain in relaxed neutral;
8. Neck remains in neutral with the chin behind the chest bone.

PREVENT PAIN BY STANDING CORRECTLY

The key is to stretch the muscles that pull you out of alignment. Then practice using the right effort of your core to hold your spine upright while relaxing your neutral back.

EXERCISE 2: HOW TO STAND WELL

When you stand practice aligning your body in 8 easy steps:

1. Stand with your feet hip-width apart and parallel;
2. Feel four corners of your feet on the ground, and ankle in neutral;
3. Lengthen your legs; do not lock your knees;
4. Find your core-supported neutral back;
5. Relax your buttocks and lengthen your tailbone so that your pelvis becomes neutral;
6. Feel your belly gently draw in toward the front of the spine allowing your spine to get taller;
7. Ideally your ears line up with your shoulders, hips, and fronts of your ankles;
8. Your chin is level. ❁

Chapter 4
Yoga Fundamentals

Who wouldn't want to feel younger and have more energy? How about a handful of work habits guaranteed to bring greater focus and efficiency so there's more time to recreate? *Yoga for Lawyers* is your answer. What if you're tormented with nagging pain? Maybe you're just plain tense. Does your brain keep going over what should have happened, what you should have done, and what new worry to worry over? If you answered yes, *Yoga for Lawyers* can help with all this and a lot more too.

This introductory handbook is a gentle approach. It's designed to not overtax your body while providing a yoga blueprint for more energy, less stress, and fewer aches and pains. It also provides recharging techniques—easy to learn mind-body things to do throughout your day to feel better so you can perform better and work smarter, getting more done in less time.

WHY DOES YOGA WORK?

When you truly relax (muscles, nervous system and brain) you can correctly stretch your body into better alignment bit by bit. Then, because you're more symmetrical, and not overly tense, you can get rid of nagging pains. You'll discover "neutral" and the body's func-tional core support necessary to sit, stand, and breathe better. Like magic you unwind, feel better, and automatically have more energy.

When you stretch in yoga, slowly, meditatively, with deep breathing, you are using your full mind focus, and therefore you are practicing a form of meditation. Meditation is famous for turning off a ruminating brain, which results in less stress and improved concentration. You think more clearly, and enjoy life more.

Your body and brain are your means of transportation to go where you want to go, and be where you want to be. So if we take the analogy of getting your car tuned up, practicing the techniques in this book will give you a brand new shiny makeover—new frame (body alignment), electrical system (brain and heart), fluids (circulatory, joint, and cranial-sacral fluid), engine (lungs and core), and a smooth ride (toned muscles, better digestion, energy, emotional balance, and confidence).

Nothing else connects the entire mind and body together which, by design, is the ultimate prescription for increased well-being. And when you feel this good you feel like moving and exercising. Bodies are designed to move. Movement and exercise turn on the chemical activities of cellular growth and repair, keeping you young. Movement and exercise are natural antidepressants, and they keep your brain sharp too. Therapeutic yoga stretching keeps bodies from getting stiff and decrepit. When you mold your bones, muscles, and joints into good alignment with yoga stretching, and use your core for good posture and movement, you will have the proper foundation to feel younger, think quicker, and feel more relaxed and pain-free.

Yoga is a different language, the language of the mind-body connection and nervous system, and it takes practice just like learning any new language. The rewards of better health in your career and your personal life last a lifetime.

HOW TO USE THE MIND-BODY TECHNIQUES IN THIS BOOK

Depending on "where you are" in your body and mind, certain chapters may be a better starting point for you:

- This chapter is a great place to start with three fundamentals: alignment, neutral, and core awareness, which are foundations for chapters 4, 5, 6, and 7.
- Get the basics of the physiology of stress with Chapter 2, and start feeling better right away by reducing stress using the relaxation techniques taught in Chapter 7.
- Use Chapter 5 for pain relief.
- Chapter 3 has tips on good posture. Chapter 6 provides recharging methods so you can get more work done in less time.
- Use Chapter 8 for meditation.
- Chapters 1 and 9 provide inspiration.

FEEL BETTER IN YOUR BODY

1. GOOD BODY ALIGNMENT GETS YOU OUT OF PAIN.

Bad posture produces back pain, and back pain is common. It's the second most common neurological ailment in the United States, second only to headaches, according to the National Institutes of Health. It's estimated that back pain that interferes with day-to-day activities affects eight out of ten people. Most people are familiar with the notion that appropriate exercise is needed to prevent back pain, but what may be less familiar is the idea that non-exercise movement and proper posture (much more involved than simply "sitting and standing up straight") are also extremely important baselines for back health, every bit as important as regular exercise.

Poor posture can cause a number of problems—poor circulation, neck and back pain, tension, stress, headaches, fatigue, digestive problems, aching joints, and cervical and lumbar compression and their related problems such as stenosis, sciatic pain, and scoliosis.

Good posture is vital. It affects the way we can function with ease as opposed to stiffness or pain. It affects emotions and self esteem. People that stand in good posture convey confidence and typically feel strong, balanced, and in charge.

We can only deprive the body of what it requires for so long before it begins to rebel against us. If you are in the majority of people with poor posture and pain, you can start to feel better right away with the therapeutic approach in this book.

Over the years, daily living causes us to adopt certain postures. If we don't realize a particular posture is unhealthy we continue to do it until it becomes a habit. That means we are habitually molded into certain shapes like slumped, round shouldered, or sway-backed. Maybe we protrude the chin forward (which strains the neck) or sit cross-legged (which torques the back). Leaning into one hip or locking our knees back as we stand puts imbalances and weaknesses in our structure.

When you are molded into postural bad habits, the rest of your body compensates for the misalignment and you end up with habitually tight and short muscles—usually on one side—producing torques and pain. By this time any attempt to sit or stand up straight will likely be impossible, and your body may be edging toward debilitating back pain related to the spine.

Core awareness is also essential to good posture. Weak and unbalanced core muscles are linked to low back pain while strong and balanced core muscles help maintain good posture and reduce strain on the spine.

This book provides a solution that addresses many root causes of back pain. By incorporating therapeutic yoga stretching, core awareness, deep relaxation, and meditation, it is possible to get out of pain, stay out of pain, and develop new good postural habits.

2. OPTIMAL STRUCTURE KEEPS YOU OUT OF PAIN.

We know the importance of diet, exercise, and emotional health, but the fourth element, structural health, has been greatly over-looked. Optimal structure and its resulting good posture is a crucial component of flexibility and staying healthy. To find structural health, first stretch your body therapeutically to improve symmetry and good alignment. When you stretch the muscles of the pelvis, legs, mid back, and shoulders, you will be able to sit and breathe better. You will also be able to stand, move, and exercise from your core, which is more readily accessed when your structure is correct.

Yoga stretching also trains you how to not tense one muscle to fight another muscle. You don't want to sustain that tension. It's like having the brake and accelerator on at the same time. For example, you will discover how to relax your chin into good posture rather than pushing it back, and how to melt your shoulders away from your ears instead of forcing them down. The quality of melting and releasing into good posture is imperative, along with alignment, neutral, and strong core support.

Your spine and trunk have a certain healthy baseline shape called "neutral" where your pelvis, ribcage, shoulder girdle, spine, neck, and head are stacked properly atop each other allowing your back to relax. Then your functional core can maintain this good posture with ease. When you breathe, your whole spine lengthens and settles. (It's the opposite of slumped, swaybacked, or tense.) Proper retraining into structural alignment allows any compressed discs to rehydrate and prevents nerves from being impinged between the vertebrae. You can easily learn to maintain neutral and elongate your spine all day, even when sitting at your desk or on the couch, or while driving or lying down. When you learn to keep the integrity of your structure intact, pain, tension, and stress will dissipate.

3. YOUR CORE SUPPORTS THE INTEGRITY OF YOUR STRUCTURE.

One of the biggest benefits of core awareness and training is to develop functional fitness, the type of fitness that is essential to daily living and regular activities. This requires an understanding of your "functional core," different from what most people think of as core strength. Your functional core does not build "six-pack" abdominals. Rather, the core consists of many of the deepest muscles in the body that run the entire length of the torso. When these muscles are properly recruited they stabilize the pelvis, spine, and shoulder girdle and create a solid base of support that allows you to stand and move in good posture while remaining relaxed. Your core distributes the stresses of weight bearing, helps your body work against the forces of gravity, and protects your back.

FEEL BETTER IN YOUR MIND

Some reasons yoga therapy works so well to de-stress and recharge you is because it releases the feel-good brain chemicals, serotonin and dopamine, as well as endorphins, all of which have a relaxing effect on your nervous system. You will also become better aware of internal body sensations. The skill of awareness is key to mastering control over the fight/flight stress response.

While most of us are more familiar with the central nervous system, it is the other nervous system—the autonomic nervous system with its sympathetic (fight/flight) and parasympathetic (relax and repair) components—that most concerns us here. Also, the vegus nerve that travels from its origin in the brain to the tongue, pharynx, vocal chords, lungs, stomach, and intestines system comes into play. This vegus nerve system has a lot to do with the stress response. Ever notice the feeling of butterflies in your gut? Hear the expression cat's got your tongue? Ever feel the hair on the back of your neck stand up? We've all felt weak knees; some of us have felt frozen like a deer in headlights. What about that knot in your stomach, your heart beating out of your chest, a clenched jaw, or your breath fast and shallow? Those are just a few examples of body sensation "stress flags" that affect speech, breathing, and digestion via the vegus nerve.

The key to maintaining a rational state of mind and lowering stress levels lies in mastering awareness of body sensations through the mind-body connection so you can realize when you are beginning to go over the edge into the stress response of the primitive brain. If you pay attention, your body will inform you that the stress chemistry of the sympathetic nervous system has been turned on. Using breath and relaxation techniques you can calm stress arousal by switching on the parasympathetic nervous system, which is in charge of relaxation and overall healing. Certain breathing techniques (for example, a 2:1 breathing ratio where your long, slow, steady exhale takes twice as long as your slow, steady inhale) often dispel stress. You cannot control the stress response at will or by will. But through the practice of yoga it is possible to better balance your nervous system and the stress response. It's easy to learn, just takes practice, and once learned can be used in the moment to keep you in your rational brain instead of getting hijacked by your primitive brain.

Every time you practice any of the numerous calming techniques in this book (therapeutic stretching, breath exercises, deep relaxation, meditation) you train yourself for better emotional resilience, which means quicker discharge of negative emotions, less stress, and a higher baseline of well-being.

GENERAL GUIDELINES

Use these fundamental concepts when practicing the exercises and yoga poses in Chapters 4, 5, 6, and 7.

1. Yoga therapy involves using the right effort: do not overextend yourself, but do push yourself the right amount.

2. Use the right amount of concentration, which means focusing on body and breath sensations in a relaxed way.

3. Find a balance between tightness and laxity, between ease and strength, between activity and relaxation. Too much tension restricts movement, uses too much energy, leads to fatigue, and places unnecessary strain on body. However with too much laxity strength and vitality are lost. The balanced end result would therefore be simultaneously relaxed, strong, and flexible.

4. When you are stretching the quality of the muscles is vitally important. Optimally they are strong, long or wide, and elastic; never rigid or hardened like steel rods.

5. Certain muscles and areas of the body are appropriately relaxed even while other muscles in the body are appropriately active and working. Nothing is forced, ever.

6. In order to receive the greatest benefits, where appropriate, square the feet, square the knees, and lift the kneecaps to straighten the legs.

7. Pay careful attention to symmetry. Placement is an important foundation which makes a difference between reinforcing a misalignment and correcting one.

8. Stretch introspectively with a dialog between your body and mind. Then you can feel which muscles need engagement versus relaxation. Yoga stretching is never stationary; you are always adjusting with micro movements, and you are always mindful of your breath. Stretching is elastic, a feeling of pulling rubber bands. It also needs to be done with the right effort—on an imaginary stretch scale the amount you stretch would be in the range of a 6 or a 7 out of a 10.

9. When your mind wanders into thoughts draw it back into your body and breath sensations.

10. Eliminate extra effort in your forehead, eyes, tongue, face, neck, jaw, throat, and shoulders.

11. Always use rhythmic breathing. Never hold your breath. Holding your breath can make you overly tense.

FUNDAMENTALS

The following awareness basics are the foundational building blocks for all succeeding chapters. These basic exercises are designed to help you find the mind-body connection, optimal structure and alignment, isolations such as engaging certain muscles with the right amount of energy while simultaneously relaxing other muscles, and certain geometric shapes. These geometric shapes are key to doing more advanced poses. Each time you practice the basics try placing your focus on one or two different general guidelines. Pretty soon all guidelines will coalesce in your mind, body, and nervous system. This is how you begin teaching yourself the new language of yoga.

By practicing neutral, functional core awareness, and core training exercises such as roll down, bridge, and plank in this chapter, you will begin to retrain yourself to sit, stand, move, and exercise better.

NEUTRAL AND CORE AWARENESS BASICS

EXERCISE 1: NEUTRAL

Let gravity and relaxation help you find your best "neutral," a shape of the bones of your back and spine that you'll use over and over again to sit and stand in good posture, as well as perform most of the yoga stretches in this book. Start by lying supine, knees bent at 90 degrees, feet hip-distance apart on the floor in parallel, and your entire back like a heavy, wide rectangle. Exhale over 10 slow, steady counts, feeling gravity. Now notice the relaxed curves of your spine—your low back vertebrae feel long, with space for a skinny pencil to slide under. Your mid-back feels flat and wide, and your neck is a graceful arc. Ideally your chin is level with your forehead. You can add a blanket or pillow under your back skull to level your chin. Notice your two pointed hipbones in the front of the pelvis are level and aimed directly up to the ceiling like the headlights of a car. Notice your low front ribs are neither flaring up toward the ceiling nor hammocking toward the ground. Raise your arms 90 degrees to the ceiling. Feel flat and wide across your shoulder blades and back. Imagine you are an upside-down table.

The following additions are basic awareness exercises to help you develop a strong, stable, central core from which all movement stems.

Add: In neutral with your arms by your sides on the ground, press into your feet and round your low back and sacrum. Feel your tailbone lift and curl up. This round shape of the low back is called a posterior tilt. Return to neutral. Now move back and forth from neutral to posterior tilt several times, with the relaxed quality of massaging your low back. Next, try tilting your pelvis in the opposite direction, into an anterior tilt, where your low back arches off the ground. Now return to neutral, which is balanced midway between posterior and anterior tilts.

Add: Lying on your back in neutral, practice lateral ribcage breathing, where your inhale fills your side ribs. Notice how your belly does not bulge up to the ceiling as your inhale sweeps wide.

Add: Find a shape called "Neutral Chair." Draw each knee up, one at a time, to place yourself in a core-supported upside-down chair. Make sure you smooth out all your low back vertebrae so they are lengthened (but not rounded) on the ground. In this way, neutral chair feels different in your low back than the neutral position. Your arms are at your sides on the ground, palms facing down. Press your hands lightly into the floor to widen your chest and support your back. Engage the pelvic floor (see Exercise 5). Keep-

4.1a Neutral

ing the 90 degree bend of your knees, exhale to engage the deep layer of abdominals, called transverse abdominals, and lower one foot to tap the ground with your big toe. Return that foot and leg to chair position on an inhale. Alternate with your opposite leg. Repeat several times, and smooth out the movement like slow-motion running. Make sure your pelvic floor and abdominal core muscles are engaged, while your shoulders and back stay relaxed in neutral. Breathe laterally in your ribcage as you carry out the movement. You'll feel the effect of deep transverse abdominal muscles drawing in toward the front of the spine, while the outer rectus abdominals do not harden. You'll also feel core muscles wrapping from your mid back around your side waists to knit your lower front ribs toward each other. (These abdominal wrap muscles stabilize your mid-back and shoulders.) Make sure you are using the "right effort" of the core. Let the work of your legs come from your core, not the muscles of your lower back. Concentrate on breathing in your ribcage and not taking tension in your head, neck, or shoulders. Be sure to keep the weight of your outer hips on the floor and the sides of your torso long. Try 10 toe taps each side.

EXERCISE 2. NEUTRAL FULL BODY STRETCH

Lie on your back with your legs fully extended along the floor and your "knees squared," i.e., the four corners of each kneecap square (like a photograph) and aimed straight up to the ceiling, and your feet "squared," i.e., flexed, in parallel, and with the outside long edge of the foot fairly even and level with the inner long edge of the foot, and the second toes straight above the center of the heels forming a 90 degree plumb line. Firm your thighs and "lift the kneecaps"

4.1b Neutral Chair

4.2 Neutral Full Body Stretch

(contract your thigh muscles to draw the kneecaps up; the correct action is to lift, not push back on the knee joints) to straighten your legs. Reach your straight arms up to the ceiling. Extend your arms overhead. Straighten your arms pressing the backs of your hands down lightly. Engage the abdominals and reach out equally through your legs from the backs of your thighs to your heels keeping your back neutral. Lengthen your side waists by reaching with your arms from your waist to your fingertips. Keep extending arms and legs in these opposite directions in a way that feels "elastic" in your muscles and spine. Maintain your pelvis in neutral. As you balance your pelvis into neutral you will also feel your buttocks muscles lengthen like they are reaching toward your feet.

Add: With arms by your sides, soften your muscles as you keep the neutral bone structure as above. This position is a good preparation to help you understand how to stand in good posture. Here the ground supports you; when you are standing your functional core will support you.

EXERCISE 3: TABLE

On hands and knees find neutral, and recruit your pelvic floor (see Exercise 5) and transverse abdominal core muscles in toward the spine with the right effort—just enough to support the flat, wide table shape of your back. (If you use too much core, your back will round or your shoulders will get tense. If you use too little core, your spine will sag.) In neutral, your shoulders slide away from your ears, and your shoulder blades are flat across your back. Core engagement does not interfere with breathing. Your ribcage breath is steady and even. Notice that when your back is in neutral your low front ribs are not dropping toward the ground.

4.3 Table

4.4 Cat Back

EXERCISE 4: CAT BACK

Start in a table position. Exhale as you lift your core abdominals into the spine and round your back in a smooth, even curve from your tailbone to your neck and crown of your head, and a smooth, even curve from your pubic bone through your throat. Be sure to use the right effort of your core—engage the pelvic floor (see Exercise 5), hollow the low belly, and pull the transverse abdominals in and up under the low front ribs. Breathe laterally in your ribcage.

EXERCISE 5: SEATED NEUTRAL

Level 1—Sit upright in neutral, bent knees, squared feet. Sit directly on the centers of your sitting bones and check (perhaps in a mirror) that you have placed your pelvis in neutral. Your front hip-bones should be level with the back rim of your pelvis. Lengthen your side waists on an inhale, and on your exhale let your breath roll over your top shoulders and down your back while your spine grows taller. This is the tall and relaxed neutral torso you will ide-ally have when sitting and standing in good posture. Now notice three bones at the bottom of your torso that form a triangle—two sitting bones and the pubic bone. The muscles inside the triangle are called the "pelvic floor." These are the bladder control muscles. They are also the gateway to the core. Practice engaging the pel-vic floor and feel a consistent lift and toning of those muscles up into the body; there should not be so much engagement of the pelvic floor that you feel tension in your back. Remember that throughout this book, all core-supported movement recruits the right effort of the pelvic floor and the deepest layer of abdominal muscle, the transverse abdominals.

Level 2—Sit upright in neutral. Stretch your legs out in front of you with your feet hip-width apart. If your hamstrings are tight, prop your buttocks on the edge of a blanket. Square your

4.5a Seated Neutral Level 1

4.5b Seated Neutral Level 2

feet, square your knees, and use your hands to align your hamstrings with a pulling/sweeping action of the hamstring muscles, inner to outer, across the backs of your legs. Engage your thigh muscles and lift your kneecaps. Stretch out your arms and check that your pelvis, spine, shoulder blades, and torso are neutral.

EXERCISE 6: ROLL DOWN

Holding onto your knees with your hands, round your low back into a posterior tilt. Continue rounding into a smooth, even C-curve shape, engaging your core—pelvic floor, navel to spine, and the transverse abdominals—in and up under the low front ribs. Relax your shoulders away from your ears and let your shoulder blades melt down your back. Practice lateral ribcage breathing while maintaining core engagement. Next, roll down, rounding and articulating each vertebra, keeping the abdominals scooped and hollowed as you make your way to the ground. To come up, roll off to one side and use your hands on the ground to push yourself to a seated position, or just grab behind your thighs and rock up to a seat. Do several roll downs before you reverse with a core-powered roll up. When rolling up, first lengthen your neck by bringing your chin slightly toward your chest, and exhale to better engage your core, which curls you up.

4.6 Roll Down

EXERCISE 7: SPHINX

The sphinx shape is a good way to learn how to extend your spine supported by your core. However, if you have a bad back, leave this one out.

Lie on your stomach with your forearms pressing into the mat. Align your elbows directly under your shoulders, and your wrists in line with your elbows. Think of lifting your upper body away from the mat by pressing up from the elbows and at the same time draw your shoulders away from your ears. Place your legs in line with your sitting bones and on the centers of the thighs. Allow the tops of your feet to press into the mat. Press your palms into the mat and slightly tip your pelvis to press the pubic bone firmly onto the ground. Feel the buttocks lengthen and your pelvis get more neutral. Draw your low belly core in to support your low back and slowly start to straighten your arms (just a little at first) while your core supports your whole spine. Over time you may be ready to fully straighten your arms. Keep your chest lifted and your neck long. Be sure to keep a lifted upper body while continuously pressing your pubic bone into the mat. When your arms are straight you can widen your collar bones, beam your sternum bone, and draw your shoulder blades closer together and down your back. Now feel a lengthening stretch of your abdomen and side waists. This full extension should be comfortable. Be careful not to sink into your shoulders or compress your low back. If your low back hurts, stop immediately and sit back on your heels in child's pose to release it.

EXERCISE 8: SEATED NEUTRAL WITH ROTATION

To find additional core muscles, practice this rotation. Sit tall and neutral with your legs stretched out straight in front of you (knees

4.7a Sphinx

4.7b Sphinx

4.8 Seated Neutral with Rotation

and feet squared, kneecaps lifting) and your arms stretched to either side of the room. Using your abdominal core and your exhale, rotate your mid and upper body to the right, staying perched on top of your hips and not moving at all in your legs or your pelvis. Notice you are keeping your pelvis squared and neutral even as you are rotating around a flagpole-like spine. Keep lifting up in the chest. Inhale as you return to your starting position. Keep your shoulders melting down. Repeat the movement to the left.

EXERCISE 9: FULL BODY ROLL DOWN
Level 1

Sit upright in neutral, straight squared knees, squared feet. Firm your thighs and "lift the kneecaps." Reach out through your legs from the backs of your thighs to your heels. Keep your legs firmly

anchored to the mat as you use your core to exhale, engaging the pelvic floor and transverse abdominals, and roll down to the ground in a smooth, even C-shaped curve, articulating each vertebra. Once on the ground, lengthen your side waists by reaching, with your arms overhead, from your waist to your fingertips. Your buttocks muscles will feel long like they are reaching toward your feet. Bend your knees, roll off to one side and use your hands on the ground to push yourself to a seat, or just grab behind your thighs and rock up to a seat. Do several roll downs before you try a roll up.

Roll up by lengthening your neck and bringing your chin toward your chest and exhaling to use your core to peel yourself up off the mat, curling forward. Use this sequence—long neck, chin toward chest, lift chest up over your ribs, lift ribs up over your belly, and lift your belly up and over your hips, and then draw yourself to a tall neutral position. Breathe steadily in the ribcage.

4.9a Seated Neutral

Level 2

Sit upright in neutral, straight squared knees, squared feet. Firm your thighs and "lift the kneecaps." Place your palms wide across the back of your skull, elbows reaching wide and shoulders melting away from your ears. Feather your head in your hands (don't pull your neck). Using an exhale to draw your core in, slowly round your spine

4.9b Full Body Roll Down Level 1

4.9c Full Body Roll Down Level 2

down to the mat. Try to feel each vertebra stretching and lengthening down as though you were putting a space between each one. The key here is to use the core incrementally. When you need the low back rounder, use more low belly core, when you place the mid vertebrae down, incrementally use more core in and up under the low front ribs, and by the time you put your back ribs down you will also feel the core muscles that wrap around your rib cage. Remember to reach strongly through the legs and buttocks, keeping the lower body glued to the mat. To come up, bend your knees, roll off to one side and use your hands on the ground to push yourself to a seat, or just grab behind your thighs and rock up to a seat.

EXERCISE 10: LYING ON THE SIDE WITH ROTATION

Start by lying on your left side, knees bent, with both arms outstretched at a 90 degree angle from your shoulders. Use your core to support your movements as you lift your straight right arm toward the ceiling, and begin to roll your chest toward the ceiling as well.

4.10 Lying on the Side with Rotation

Your right arm will continue a sweeping arc movement across the ceiling and toward the ground as you simultaneously revolve your upper body. Go slow and revolve a comfortable amount. Reverse and try the second side.

EXERCISE 11: BRIDGE

Lie on your back in neutral with your knees bent, hip-width apart, and the soles of your feet on the mat in parallel. Using your core, round your low back and sacrum into a posterior tilt, then peel each vertebra up off the mat in succession until you are a neutral "bridge". Lift your arms 90 degrees up to the ceiling, then stretch your arms overhead. Using your core, articulate your spine back to the ground. Try to feel each vertebra stretching and lengthening as though you were putting a space between each one. The muscles alongside your spine and your side waists become elastic as you round down, touching your low back first (posterior tilt) before you return to neutral. Bring your arms back up to the ceiling and down by your sides.

4.11a Bridge

4.11b Bridge

4.11c Bridge

4.11d Bridge

4.11e Bridge

4.11f Bridge

EXERCISE 12: PLANK

Kneel on all fours (table position). Double-check your core engagement. Step one foot behind you, toes tucked under, and straighten the back leg. Double check you are still in neutral and core-supported. Move your second leg back so you are in a push-up or plank position. Make sure your buttocks are in a straight line with your spine. You become a long straight rod from your head to your heels. Stretch through your inner heels, and firm both thighs. Push the floor away with your hands keeping your arms straight. Reach through the crown of the head and keep the shoulder tops away from the ears and the shoulder blades flat. Hold for 10–20 seconds breathing evenly.

Back Leg Lift—From a plank position maintain your core and lift one leg straight off the mat on an exhale, keep breathing in the ribcage as you hold your leg in the air, then exhale again as you return to plank position. Switch legs. Throughout the exercise keep your arms and legs completely straight and think of pushing up and away from the heels of your hands so you do not sink into your wrists.

4.12b Plank

4.12a Plank

4.12c Plank (plank into back leg lift)

EXERCISE 13: NEUTRAL SCISSORS

The core abdominals draw in and abdominal wrap muscles knit around your ribs from back to front. Move from your core, scissoring your legs and keeping your back neutral.

EXERCISE 14: NEUTRAL LEG LIFTS AND LOWERS

This exercise gives you the core awareness and strength to keep your spine long in an upright or standing position. With strong core muscles you can sit and stand up tall with a lift in the center of your body. (Without core strength the rib cage starts to sink toward the pelvis and the shoulders and head can get pulled forward causing tension in the upper back.)

Practice reaching the legs up to the ceiling at 90 degrees (perpendicular to the floor), keeping the back neutral and the outer hips in contact with the floor. Align your feet and legs; knees can bend if needed. You should use some core just to stay neutral. Now use more core, on an exhale, to lower your legs toward the ground to about 45 degrees; then lift your legs up toward the ceiling to 90 degrees on an inhale. Do several rounds slowly with control, all the while staying neutral and stable in your back and powering from your core. As you lift your legs, do not let them swing toward your face beyond 90 degrees. As you lower your legs, draw your lower belly in a lot more and lengthen your low back and buttocks toward your heels. Use your entire core to stay neutral through the exercise, including the muscles that wrap around your ribcage, and never hold your breath. When you are practicing leg lowers and lifts, maintain ease in your hip flexors, inner groin, and low back. When you get really competent, you may want to lower your legs a little further down while staying neutral. ✳

4.13 Neutral Scissors

4.14a Neutral Leg Lift

4.14b Neutral Leg Lift

4.1a Neutral, 4.1b Neutral Chair   4.2 Neutral Full Body Stretch   4.3 Table   4.4 Cat Back

4.5a Seated Neutral Level 1, 4.5b Seated Neutral Level 2   4.6 Roll Down   4.7a Sphinx, 4.7b Sphinx

4.8 Seated Neutral with Rotation   4.9a Seated Neutral, 4.9b Full Body Roll Down Level 1, 4.9c Full Body Roll Down Level 2   4.10 Lying on the Side with Rotation

4.11a Bridge, 4.11b Bridge, 4.11c Bridge, 4.11d Bridge, 4.11e Bridge, 4.11f Bridge

4.12a Plank, 4.12b Plank, 4.12c Plank (plank into back leg lift)   4.13 Neutral Scissors   4.14a Neutral Leg Lift, 4.14b Neutral Leg Lift

5

Rx Yoga Therapy: Relief for Backs and Shoulders

Do you leave work with your back screaming for a massage? Is your belly tight with tension or your jaw clenched? Are you very, very stiff and cringe with even the simplest stretch? Maybe annoying pains keep you awake at night. Use this chapter for relief. Rx yoga therapy is a terrific way to eliminate uncomfortable tensions, pain, and stress, and it is also a remarkable preventative solution.

INTRODUCTION TO Rx YOGA THERAPY

This chapter is written for those of you who don't want to do the strenuous classic poses other yoga books illustrate.

Here is a program anyone can easily perform—doable yoga shapes to stretch your body into symmetry. The stretches here are easy to do yet still physically challenging. Many are pre-yoga poses.

There are reasons many lawyers experience physical pain. Body torques and misalignments due to poor posture and stress are common. Whether you are experiencing throbbing, twinges, pinching, aching or the resulting brain fog that often accompanies chronic pain, you are bound to feel immediate physical relief and mental alertness when you practice Rx yoga therapy.

Most nagging types of pain in the back and shoulders are muscular and related to misalignments. In this chapter, detailed instructions will guide you to your mind-body connection where your body and nervous system start to heal the pain. In a relaxed state of mind you'll bathe yourself in the resultant feel-good brain-body chemicals: dopamine, which lights up the learning centers in the brain, and serotonin, which calms and relaxes you. Since tight muscles pull your bones (including your vertebrae) out of alignment, the geometric yoga shapes will teach you how to stack your bones into alignment. You will learn how to stretch your muscles with your bones stacked properly so you can line up your entire structure including your joints in correct alignment for good posture throughout your day. Good posture provides the proper foundation for optimal biomechanics in movement and pain-free living.

One of the main culprits of back pain for lawyers is sitting. Sitting too long at a time, hunching over, using your mouse, and typing for hours, slumping, rounding, or arching your low back in your chair, rounding your shoulders, thrusting your head and neck forward, and shouldering a phone to your ear all contribute to misalignments and pain. Crossing your legs puts a spiral of torques through your whole body. All in all sitting in these contorted ways is a recipe for chronic pain. It's important to stretch your way into good alignment so you can sit in better posture.

Rx yoga therapy will also give you awareness of associations throughout your body that contribute to relief from pain, providing you with more awareness of how to stay out of pain. Here are a few examples:

If you experience the misalignment of kyphosis (rounded shoulders, tense neck), overly tight muscles in the front of your body collapse your chest and shorten your neck. When you stretch yourself so your bones can stack up into correct alignment, you'll notice relief and less tension in your shoulders, chest, and your neck as those areas are freed to line up properly. And your lung capacity will improve as you take full breaths for the first time in a long time.

Maybe you have stiff hamstrings? Because the hamstring muscles at the backs of your thighs are attached to your sitting bones, when they are tight they pull on your pelvis causing misalignment and pain in your back, hips, or knees. If these areas hurt, you can help relieve the pain by stretching your hamstrings.

Sitting causes the hip flexors (muscles that draw the thighs up to the torso) to shorten and no longer accommodate full movement in the hip socket (which in turn retards the flow of the synovial fluid that lubricates the joint, increasing the chance of calcium buildup). To avoid hip replacement surgery, make sure you stretch your hip flexors and other muscles in your pelvis for hip health.

Tightened hip flexors also contribute to swayback posture, which compresses the low back vertebrae and hunches the shoulders. Alleviate the resultant pain at both ends of your spine with therapeutic alignment through stretching properly.

The therapeutic approach in this chapter is based on the science of yoga and its universal principles of alignment as well as on modern exercise science and modern brain science. An effective way to stretch and relieve pain, Rx yoga therapy is not jerky or forced. There is no bouncing or yanking (which actually shortens muscles). Rather it is slow and controlled. The slowness gives the practitioner great control over the precise positioning instructed. Rx yoga therapy uses geometrical shapes that promote physical symmetry and freedom from torques and pain. Within these easy-to-do shapes the practitioner is invited to notice what's tight, what's short, what's tense, in other words what's causing the pain. By careful attention to placement of your bones, you will discover how misalignments have caused you to become weak or tight, twisted or torqued. You will be able to stretch the short or tight places with your breath. Soon pain will dissipate and certain aberrations that used to feel normal will not feel right anymore as you experience correct alignment. This is how the new good alignment can start to become the norm.

Don't be fooled by the static pictures here. Let me assure you, there are no stagnant moments, no stationary posing when you are stretching yourself with Rx yoga therapy. With every breath there are micro movements throughout your body as you locate imbalances and make adjustments. While stretching, your mind-body connection is fully utilized as your attention is directed to your front, back, sides, limbs, joints, and muscles. Your breath helps you notice tight, painful places and your nervous system and mind focus help release pain. You'll discover that your conscious breath travels to where you place your mind focus and produces more blood flow and stretch in the right places. Blood delivers the body's repair chemicals and also hydrates tight, locked or frozen muscles providing more suppleness. This intimate connection between the mind and the body is the essence of yoga therapy.

You are most likely looking for a particular result—to soothe your aching back or shoulders—and are motivated to solve your problem. Therefore the instructions for each pose are quite detailed. When you practice the poses a couple of times with careful attention to all the instructions, your body and nervous system will learn the correct way to do them and you won't have to continue reading all the instructions in future practice sessions.

There is also a certain precision needed in order to obtain optimal alignment. Meticulously follow the placement directions. This information is the foundation and the basis for the balancing effects that good alignment provides. For example, the seemingly small action of squaring your feet has profound alignment implications into your hips, which in turn provides more symmetry in your entire pelvis and spine. (If you walk with your feet turned out and stretch with your feet turned out you will likely reinforce a misalignment. If the foundation is placed incorrectly, the benefits of the pose are lost.)

Yoga therapy retrains your mind to focus on one thing. When you focus on body sensations and your breath, stretching becomes a form of meditation.

When you are pain free you are more able to be calm, centered, and able to make better decisions.

An added benefit of greater symmetry through good alignment is that when there is less pain there is less stress. While it's true that stress and worry are additional culprits of body tensions resulting in pain, it's also true that poor body mechanics also puts more tensions and pain patterns into your body, which results in additional stress.

Yoga therapy provides increased muscular flexibility, which prevents common injuries.

There may be a calmness and overall increase in well-being underlying your daily life from the relaxation that you feel while stretching, and from the relaxation you feel after stretching, and from the relaxation you get from practicing good alignment throughout your day.

You will probably feel younger.

In time you will not have to decide logically where you need to stretch; you will be able to feel what needs attention.

Because stretching in good alignment naturally creates more awareness and mind-body connection, pretty soon you may be incorporating good body alignments in all your activities, from sitting to standing and all movement including sports or exercise.

MORE BENEFITS FROM Rx YOGA THERAPY

Yoga therapy undoes muscle knots that sap your energy and wear away at your nervous system.

WAYS TO DO Rx YOGA THERAPY

You can do Chapter 5 as a warm-up routine (once you've learned it, it takes approximately 30 minutes to do the whole thing) or you can use the individual poses for pain relief or mini-breaks during your day. For example, lie on the foam roller for 1–2 minutes every couple hours in order to re-align and de-stress.

> As you practice yoga therapy your body will become more aligned and pains will start to disappear, especially when you pay attention to good alignment while sitting, standing, and moving throughout your day.

GENERAL GUIDELINES FOR PRACTICING Rx YOGA

For diagnosed injuries or severe pain, the place to start is with your medical practitioner. When you get the okay consider starting your yoga practice with Chapter 7 relaxation before proceeding with this chapter.

Hold poses as long as comfortable—usually 10–20 seconds to start. Use the right effort of core support in all the poses. Good alignment cannot be rushed or forced. Never force your body into alignment before your tissue has adjusted—i.e., do not suddenly change the way your feet or knees point while standing when it's a pattern that is in every bone ligament and fiber of your musculoskeletal system. Rather, practice squaring up the knees and feet while in the seated yoga poses and with regular practice the new alignments will automatically start to slip into your body for use in standing.

Your degree of flexibility does not determine success. Rather, success in yoga therapy is measured by your inward attention and the reduction and elimination of your pain.

Never do any pose that causes pain. Use your breath to enhance stretching.

How to do forward bends correctly: Keep the feet active and squared, so the inner edges of the feet are parallel with the outer edges, square the knees, and lift the kneecaps by firming the thighs. Consider the torso as a single unit and bend from the hips with your back in neutral. Keep your head in line with your spine. Keep your throat, neck, jaw, and shoulders soft and relaxed.

Move slowly. When movement is slow you can feel which muscles are working, which muscles need to relax, and which part of your body needs your attention.

How far to stretch? Go as far into the pose as you can while comfortably maintaining the correct alignment—where you feel sensation but not pain.

Eliminate extra effort. Activate only those muscles, including core, necessary for the pose. Notice and release tensions in all other muscles including your eyes, face, neck, jaw, throat, and shoulders.

If you have heart disease or hypertension that is not controlled by medication, keep your head above your heart and don't elevate your legs above your heart.

Whenever possible breathe in and out through your nose—this air is filtered and warmed and this allows relaxation of your head and jaw.

In general keep your eyes open to practice being in the outer world while noticing inner sensations. The occasional use of a full-length mirror is often useful to check your alignment.

Whenever beneficial, allow your forehead to recede, imagine your eyes dropping to the backs of your eye sockets, and allow your tongue to relax, especially at the back, as it melts away from the roof of your mouth. These actions release excess tension throughout the body.

Rx YOGA FOR BACK, SHOULDERS, OVERALL PAIN, AND STRESS

This chapter describes stretches that will help ease your back and shoulders and other pains. Any of the poses can be adapted for an office stretch break with office doors closed.

EXERCISE 1: FOAM ROLLER

Props needed: a standard foam roller, 6 inches in diameter, and a folded blanket to pad the roller (optional) in case the roller feels too hard or your back feels tender.

The passive stretch and the linear position of your spine on the foam roller help you relax and discover good alignment.

Sit at the end of a six-inch diameter standard foam roller. Place your hands on the ground to support you as you round your sacrum and low back and gently draw your low belly core in. Round your spine to touch your sacrum and each low back vertebra in succession onto the roll and keep rounding down until all your vertebrae and your back skull rests on the roller. Relax your shoulders and allow your shoulder blades to drape over the roll. Relax your pelvis and notice that your mid-back vertebrae are still touching the roll and only something as small as a pencil could slide under your low back.

Close your eyes and focus on a long exhale breath (perhaps 10 counts) and on the body sensations of sinking into the roll. Allow your forehead to recede, imagine your eyes dropping to the backs of your eye sockets, and allow your tongue to relax, especially at the back, as it melts away from the roof of your mouth. Continue for five–ten slow steady exhales. Next, practice focusing on your inhales, allowing your side ribs to expand sideways on each breath. (On an inhale your low belly will draw in towards the front of the spine as the ribs expand away from the spine.) Next, expand the side and the back ribs. Lastly, allow one full breath to travel to the side and back ribs, then all the way up to your top chest, across your shoulder blades and up to your top shoulders for a full 360-degree breath. Repeat as many rounds as desired. Let your exhales release any body tensions.

When complete, slide off your roller onto your mat, and arrange your back in neutral with your knees bent and the soles of your feet flat on the ground in parallel. Memorize the sensation of your back in neutral so you can replicate this shape in many of your poses.

5.1 Foam Roller

EXERCISE 2: SHOULDER BLADE MASSAGE WITH THIGH STRETCH

Props needed: a standard foam roller, 6 inches in diameter. This exercise massages tight shoulder muscles and relaxes the neck.

Rest your head in your hands. Relax your neck and throat muscles. As you roll to the bottom of your shoulder blades, your back rounds and your face looks at your knees. As you roll to the top of your shoulders, your back straightens out while your face looks at the ceiling. Continue rolling and melting your shoulder muscles as though you are kneading dough.

5.2 Shoulder Blade Massage

EXERCISE 3: SEATED BOUND ANGLE

This pose creates ideal spinal alignment and stretches the low back, hips, and inner thighs.

In a seated neutral back position create a straight vertical line with your spine as you press the soles of your feet together bending your knees out to the sides. Using muscles in the pelvis, gently pull your inner thighs wide. If you can easily keep your spine straight, place your hands on the ground behind your hips and hinge forward from your hips at a diagonal. Elongate your spine as you keep your chest lifted and the back of your neck long.

5.3 Seated Bound Angle

EXERCISE 4: SEATED FORWARD BEND

Optional props: a blanket, a block, and a strap.

This pose lengthens the spine, and stretches the back.

If your hamstrings are tight, prop your buttocks up on the edge of a blanket. Stretch out your legs in front of you with your feet hip-width apart and squared. (Optional—position a block against the soles of your feet. Loop a strap around the block, holding one side of the strap in each hand. Square your feet into the block.) Also square your knees to the ceiling. Use your hands at the backs of your legs to align your hamstrings with a pulling/sweeping action of the muscles inner to outer across the backs of your legs. Engage your thigh muscles above the kneecaps to firm and straighten the legs. Check to see that your back and pelvis are neutral before hinging forward. If not, add more blankets for greater height to avoid pulling in the low back. Hinge forward from the hips elongating your spine in a straight diagonal over your legs while keeping your chest lifted and the back of your neck long.

To add more stretch if your body is ready, gently hinge forward with straight spine before rounding your spine into an even curve, from tailbone to back skull. Your knees can slightly bend if necessary. When you are in the pose, your sitting bones widen and your tailbone draws under. As you slowly fold into this deeper forward bend, observe the muscles of your back letting go and your mind turning inward. Relax your forehead, eyes, and tongue. Focus your mind on at a tight area as you imagine your breath going directly there. To come out of the pose, use your hands on the ground to slowly bring your spine back to vertical with as much elongation as possible.

5.4a Seated Forward Bend Level 1

5.4b Seated Forward Bend Level 2

EXERCISE 5: SEATED PIGEON

Props needed: a block.

This pose stretches the outer thighs and hips.

Stretch your legs out in front of you with your feet squared. With your back in neutral, cross your right ankle over your left thigh just above the left knee. Place your right ankle on a low level block, keeping your foot and ankle aligned. Use your hands on the ground to help you keep your spine long and straight, your sitting bones grounded, and your pelvis square and level. Repeat on the other side.

For a deeper hip-opening position, add hinging forward from the hips at a diagonal with a neutral back.

EXERCISE 6: SEATED WIDE LEGS

This pose lengthens the spine, and stretches the back and the inner thighs.

If your hamstrings are tight, prop your buttocks on the edge of a blanket. Stretch your legs in a V-shape with your feet squared. Line up a vertical plumb line of your second toes directly over your heels. Use your hands at the backs of your legs to realign your hamstrings by a pulling/sweeping action of the muscles inner to outer across the backs of your legs. Square your knees to the ceiling. Engage the thigh muscles above the kneecaps to straighten the legs. Check to see that your torso is neutral and vertical. If not, add more blankets for greater height to avoid pulling in the low back. Use your breath to lift yourself taller on your inhale.

For additional stretch, hinge forward in neutral from your hips at a diagonal keeping your chest lifted and the back of your neck long. Next, gently fold forward and round your spine into an

5.5 Seated Pigeon

5.6a Seated Wide Legs Level 1

even curve, from tailbone to back skull, as you walk your hands farther out in front of you to gently stretch the backs of your legs. Your knees can slightly bend if necessary. When you are in the pose, your sitting bones widen, your buttocks lengthen toward the ground, and your tailbone draws under.

To come out of the pose, use your hands on the ground to slowly bring your spine back to vertical with as much elongation as possible.

For additional stretch of your right and left low back, keep your pelvis on the ground as though you are sitting on a heavy throne. Keep your sitting bones in contact with the floor, acting as anchors. Look toward your right foot as you slightly rotate right and bring your chest closer to your right thigh. Push your right hand on the ground to help you press your left sitting bone down. Inhale while imagining that your left low back is reaching behind you and your spine is reaching the opposite direction (like pulling a rubber band in two directions). To come out of the pose, use your hands on the ground to slowly bring your spine back to center. Repeat on the other side.

5.6b Seated Wide Legs Level 2

EXERCISE 7: THREAD THE NEEDLE

This pose lengthens the side waists and stretches the arms (including the deltoids) and the shoulders.

From table position make sure you keep your core to support your spine as you rotate your mid-back and place your outer right shoulder on the ground, arm outstretched, palm up. (Your spine stays linear right down the middle of your mat, your pelvis stays level, your ribs do not droop and your hips remain over your knees.) Your left arm reaches overhead in line with your left side

5.7 Thread the Needle

waist, palm down. Focus on lengthening your side waists with your inhale breath. Then change your focus to stretch wide across your shoulder blades on your inhale breath. Repeat on the other side.

EXERCISE 8: LONG CHILD'S POSE

This pose stretches and relaxes the pelvis, lengthens the side waists, and stretches the shoulders and arms.

From table position, place your shins on the ground on their centerlines and align your ankles and feet. Press with your hands to lower your buttocks rounding your low back and pelvis toward your heels as your arms stretch out in front of you. Rest your forehead at the hairline on the ground or on a block or blanket. Imagine your tailbone heavy like an anchor. Your inhale breath creates more space between each vertebrae. Continue breathing your spine long.

5.8 Long Child's Pose

EXERCISE 9: PUPPY INTO DOG POSE

This pose stretches the side waists, shoulders, and hamstrings.

From table position press into your palms and lift your pelvis over your ankles with your knees very bent. (Your belly will come close to your thighs.) Keep your core to support your neutral back. This is Puppy Pose. Slowly start to straighten your knees and lower your heels. Your body will form a straight line from your wrists to your hips.) This is Dog Pose. Relax your head and neck and firm your thighs. Continue to press into your hands lengthening your spine.

5.9 Puppy Into Dog Pose

EXERCISE 10: FOREARM DOG POSE

Props needed: a block (optional).

This pose teaches proper shoulder alignment.

Place a low level horizontal block on your mat. Place your forearms on the ground, palms touching the outside edges of the block. Position your shoulders directly above your elbows and keep them there throughout. (Take care to line up your wrists in a straight line with your inner elbows, and your inner elbows in a straight line with your inner armpits.) Press your palms into the block and press your outer wrists into the ground. Slightly draw your elbows toward the midline while relaxing your top shoulders away from your ears. Notice your biceps face straight forward and your triceps face straight back. Notice how flat and wide you are across your shoulder blades. Tuck your toes under and lift your pelvis into Puppy Dog (knees stay bent) or Dog Pose. Your shoulders stay directly above your elbows. To come out of the pose use more core to lower your knees to the ground and rest in child's pose.

For additional stretch and alignment of the lower arms (which affects your shoulders) try the pose again, but this time put your palms flat on the ground, surrounding the block with your thumbs at the lower edge of the block and your index fingers at the sides of the block. Rise into Dog Pose. This time press your inner wrists toward the ground. Feel your lower arm muscles wrap around the bones.

5.10 Forearm Dog Pose

5.11a Pigeon Pose Level 1

EXERCISE 11: PIGEON POSE

This pose stretches the hips and hip flexors.

From table position place your right shinbone flat on the ground at a diagonal across your mat and place your right ankle in front of your left thigh and hipbone. Align your right foot and ankle (top of foot faces the ground, sole of the foot faces the ceiling). Hips stay level as you slide your left leg back in space in line with your left sitting bone. Notice your torso is in a core-supported table shape with your two front hipbones level and pointed straight down. Rest your forehead on your stacked hands.

For additional hip stretch, keep the table shape of your back as you tuck your left toes under, lift your left knee, firm your left leg and reach your left heel straight back. Use the ball of your foot on the ground to position your hamstrings flat to the ceiling keeping

5.11b Pigeon Pose Level 2

5.11c Pigeon Pose Level 3

your pelvis level. Breathe width across your hips and buttocks and length on your left side. To come out of the pose reverse the actions and repeat on your other side.

For a hip flexor stretch place the top of your back foot back on the ground and use more core to support your low back as you lift your torso toward vertical.

EXERCISE 12: KNEELING INNER THIGH/HIP FLEXOR STRETCH

This pose stretches the inner thighs and hip flexors.

Kneel and bring one leg forward at a 90-degree angle (front knee directly over your ankle) and your front foot directly in line with your sitting bone. You may keep your fingertips on the ground or on blocks for stability. Keeping your torso fairly erect and your back in neutral slowly bring your pubic bone forward in space. Make sure to keep balanced, neutral, and lifted out of gravity by using your core. Keep

your feet, ankles, knees, and hips lined up with your sitting bones and keep your hips level. Release and practice on your opposite side.

For additional stretch, place your hands on your front knee and raise your torso upright, supporting yourself with your core.

EXERCISE 13: RUNNER'S LUNGE

This pose stretches the inner thighs and strengthens the core, legs, and back.

Begin in Kneeling Inner Thigh Stretch with one leg forward at a 90-degree angle (knee directly over the ankle). Place your fingertips on the floor or on blocks outside your foot. Turn the toes of your back foot under. Straighten and firm your back leg. Lift the back kneecap and keep your pelvis square and your side waists equally long (i.e., neutral). Lengthen through the back inner heel. Gently stretch both inner thighs wider apart like pulling a rubber band in two directions. Release and practice on the opposite side.

5.12a Kneeling Inner Thigh/Hip Flexor Stretch
Level 1

5.12b Kneeling Inner Thigh/Hip Flexor Stretch
Level 2

5.13 Runner's Lunge

5.14 Plank Pose

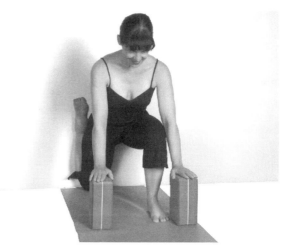

5.15 Thigh Stretch

EXERCISE 14: PLANK POSE

This pose strengthens the core, arms, shoulders, and back.

Kneel on all fours (table position). Check that all 10 fingers point directly forward with shoulders in line with wrists. Double-check your core engagement. Step one foot behind you with toes tucked under and straighten and firm the back leg. Move your second leg back so you are in a plank position, with your buttocks in line with your spine. Stretching back through your inner heels, firm both thighs. Push the floor away with your hands as you straighten your arms. Stretch through the crown of the head and keep the shoulders drawing away from the ears. As much as possible, and without force, face the biceps slightly forward and face the triceps slightly backward and keep the inner elbows aligned and slightly drawing in toward the midline.

EXERCISE 15: THIGH STRETCH

Props needed: a wall, 2 blocks.

This pose stretches the thighs.

Place your right knee close to a wall and position your shin up the wall. The top of your foot will touch the wall. If this is too much thigh stretch, place your knee father away from the wall, and press the ball of your foot into the wall. Instead of putting pressure on the knee itself, position your knee so that the pressure is on the muscle above the kneecap. Keep your hips level, use your core, and place your left leg in a runner's lunge position. Hands are on tall blocks for support. Slowly bring your spine upright as you engage your low belly core to position your tailbone and buttocks more neutrally, while keeping your hips level. Release and practice on the opposite side.

EXERCISE 16: SIDE BEND

This pose stretches the side waists (which tend to become restricted due to collapsed posture) and also provides greater mobility in the abdominal oblique muscles, which allows for greater ease in breathing.

Seated in a "mermaid" position, with your legs crossed to your right, take your left arm above your head. Stretch through your fingers keeping your arm strong. Exhale and side bend to the right keeping your ribs and shoulder blades neutral. Switch sides.

EXERCISE 17: RECLINING HAMSTRING STRETCH

Props needed: a wall (optional) and a strap.

This pose stretches the hamstrings and calves while protecting the back.

On your back in neutral, knees bent and feet on the floor, bend your right leg in toward your chest and place a strap around the ball of your foot. Slide your left leg to be straight on the ground, aligned, hips level, and your back in neutral. Extend through the right inner heel as you keep (as much as possible without force) the foot, ankle, and knee aligned. Continue to straighten the right leg, inching out more hamstring stretch while you keep your hips square and level. Release slowly and practice the opposite side.

5.16 Side Bend

5.17 Reclining Hamstring Stretch

EXERCISE 18: RECLINING INNER THIGH STRETCH

Props needed: a wall (optional), a block, and a strap.

This pose stretches the inner thighs.

Start in Reclining Hamstring Stretch on the left side. Place the strap in your left hand. Lower your left leg to the side, foot onto a block while keeping your back neutral and both sides of your pelvis and entire torso on the ground. Place your right hand on your right front hipbone to press it toward the ground and away from your left wide leg. Use your breath to create a feeling of width across the front of the pelvis. Bring your wide leg back to center before switching sides.

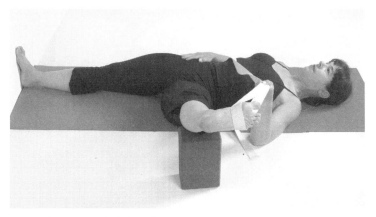

5.18 Reclining Inner Thigh Stretch

EXERCISE 19: RECLINING OUTER THIGH STRETCH

Props needed: a wall (optional), and a strap.

This pose stretches the outer lateral hamstrings.

Start in Reclining Hamstring Stretch on the right side. Place the strap in the left hand. Slightly bring your right leg toward the left (approximately 12"–18" off the center midline) while keeping your back neutral and both sides of your pelvis on the ground. (Tip: if you find your right side of your pelvis starts to roll up off the ground, use your right thumb in the right hip crease to pull the right side of the pelvis down toward the ground and to also pull the right hip crease away from your head which helps square your pelvis.) Bring your right leg back to center before switching sides.

5.19 Reclining Outer Thigh Stretch

EXERCISE 20: SUPPORTED UPPER BACK EXTENSION— THREE VERSIONS

Props needed: a thin rolled blanket and a wall.

These poses stretch muscles for aligned shoulder posture using the floor and a wall as a reference. They emphasize freeing and releasing the upper chest while giving extra feedback on proper placement of the shoulders. They also release the mid-back and stretch the side waists.

Passive stretch—Place a thin blanket roll under your shoulder blades. Recline on the prop, positioning the roll just beneath the shoulder blades across your upper back. Bend your arms to right angles, palms up. Your neck should be soft and in its smooth natural curve. If your low back is uncomfortable, bend your knees with your feet on the floor, wider than your hips, and let your knees rest together. Ease the buttocks toward your heels lengthening your low back. If your neck is uncomfortable, use a thinner roll under your shoulders and place another blanket under your head for more support. Breathe into your upper back and shoulders, feeling your shoulder blades expand into the blanket roll on your inhale.

Side Waists Stretch—From Passive Stretch position, straighten and firm your legs keeping your feet, ankles, and knees in alignment. Lift your arms up to the ceiling, clasp your elbows, and reach your arms overhead. Feel your side waists elongate on your inhales.

Shoulder Alignment Stretch—Put a thin blanket roll far enough away from a wall so that when you extend your arms overhead your hands can press into the wall. Recline onto the prop, positioning the roll just beneath the shoulder blades across your upper back. Straighten and firm your legs keeping your feet, ankles, and knees in alignment. Reach your arms up to the ceiling and then overhead. Position your palms pressing on the wall slightly higher than shoulder height with your wrist creases level and your fingers pointing down. Straighten your arms slowly and feel your shoulder tops gliding toward your feet as you lengthen your side waists. (Tip: your neck should be soft and in its smooth natural curve; if your neck is uncomfortable, use a thinner blanket roll under your shoulders and place another blanket under your head for more support.)

5.20a Passive Stretch

5.20b Side Waists Stretch

5.20c Shoulder Alignment Stretch

EXERCISE 21: SEATED HERO'S POSE WITH OVERHEAD ARM STRETCH

Props needed: one or two blocks (optional).

This seated pose stretches and balances alignment in the following areas: lower legs and ankles, thighs, side waists, shoulders, chest, and arms. The pose also teaches neutral pelvis (important to understand therapeutic sitting).

Kneel on all fours (table position). Take care to position your shinbones flat on the floor and align your ankles. Stretch your feet straight back lining up your second toes (soles of the feet facing the ceiling) with your center heels as much as possible without putting strain in any joint including your ankles and knees. Sit your buttocks on one (or two stacked) low level horizontally placed blocks. (You can remove the blocks and sit on the floor between your feet if your knees and ankles are fine.) Sit in neutral on the centers of your sitting bones. Lengthen your tailbone, buttocks, and low back vertebrae noticing how those actions bring your pelvis more neutral (as opposed to an anterior tilt). Do not pull your low belly in muscularly, but do notice that your low belly automatically draws in because of your neutral structure alone. (This awareness is important for therapeutic sitting, Chapter 3.) Imagine your breath starting at the top of your pelvis. Let your inhale stretch your side waists up like a slinky even as your shoulders remain relaxed away from your ears. Keep the length in your trunk as you let your breath roll over your top shoulders and down your back like warm bath water on your exhale. Simultaneously notice your neck and crown of your head lengthening toward the ceiling on your exhale. Try three long, slow breaths keeping your back and pelvis in neutral. Interlace your fingers (palms facing you) in front of your chest and turn your hands to press your palms facing away from you. Straighten your arms in front of your chest. Keep neutral through your back, pelvis and ribs as you lift your arms overhead in slow motion and press your palms toward the ceiling. Soften your face and throat and neck. Breathe high into the chest and lift the spine with each inhalation. Release and switch the interlace of your fingers to do the opposite side.

5.21a Seated Hero's Pose

5.21b Seated Hero's Pose with Overhead Arm Stretch

EXERCISE 22: SEATED HERO'S POSE WITH HANDCLASP SHOULDER STRETCH

This pose is especially beneficial for those with rounded shoulders and collapsed chests.

Sit in Hero's Pose. Roll your shoulders, up, back, and down the back. Place your palms on the back of your pelvis, fingers pointing down. Draw your shoulder blades and bent elbows closer together. Interlace your fingers. (Feel your collar bones widen.) Relax your shoulder tops away from your ears. Straighten your arms with your hands at buttocks height. If comfortable draw your palms toward each other. If comfortable raise your arms slightly. Soften your face and throat and neck. Relax the muscles around the shoulder blades. Breathe high into the chest and shoulders and lift the spine with each inhalation. Release and switch the interlace of your fingers to do the opposite side.

5.22 Seated Hero's Pose with Handclasp Shoulder Stretch

EXERCISE 23: SHOULDER BLADE STRETCH

This pose stretches the upper back and shoulders including the muscles underneath the shoulder blades.

Sit aligned in any comfortable position, including cross-legged pose (shown here) or hero's pose. Bend your elbows and cross your left elbow over the right fitting it snugly into the notch of the right elbow so that both elbows are directly in front of your chest with your forearms and fingers stretching up and your thumbs facing your head. Place your palms together. (If your palms don't touch simply keep the backs of the hands gently drawing toward each other.) Raise your elbows to shoulder level while lowering your top shoulders away from your ears. Inhale to broaden the muscles of the shoulder blade area wide across the back toward the outer shoulders. Release and switch sides.

5.23 Shoulder Blade Stretch

EXERCISE 24: WATERFALL

From standing position with feet, ankles, and knees in alignment, fold forward, core supported, perhaps bending your knees slightly and feeling like a rag doll in your torso. Your low belly hollows and your shoulders, neck, and head hang, relaxing the muscles. As your low back and waist release, feel your spine and side waists pour from your pelvis like a waterfall on your inhale breath. Clasp the elbows. Keep your knees bent or slowly straighten your legs. Use your core to slowly roll up, or bend your knees and press your hands into your thighs to come up.

5.24 Waterfall

EXERCISE 25: ENDING POSE

This pose creates deep relaxation to ensure that your muscles and all the nerve endings throughout your body that have been stretched and re-aligned now have time to settle down and adjust to their new configuration. Resting, even for a couple of minutes after your stretch session, will help ensure that your muscles will not clamp down and that you will re-enter your day relaxed and revitalized.

Start seated, knees bent, feet flat on the floor. Slowly round down through the spine with each vertebra landing in succession right down the middle. Either keep your knees bent or extend your legs out in front of you. In this pose, your back and pelvis are neutral and your limbs are relaxed and equidistant from your trunk. Your palms are up, and your shoulder blades are heavy with relaxation and melted flush against the floor. Your chin and forehead are at equal height. Use a long, slow exhale to release all unnecessary tensions in your forehead, eyes, tongue, jaw, shoulders, arms, torso, and legs. While your body lets go, your mind stays alert. As you take a break from external movement, allow your mind to

5.25 Ending Pose

become acutely sensitive to internal sensations. Notice a heightened awareness, and as thoughts roll in, bring your attention back to your breath and body sensations. ❋

5.1 Foam Roller

5.2 Shoulder Blade Massage

5.3 Seated Bound Angle

5.4a Seated Forward Bend Level 1, 5.4b Seated Forward Bend Level 2

5.5 Seated Pigeon

5.6a Seated Wide Legs Level 1, 5.6b Seated Wide Legs Level 2

5.7 Thread the Needle

5.8 Long Child's Pose

5.9 Puppy Into Dog Pose

5.10 Forearm Dog Pose

5.11a Pigeon Pose Level 1, 5.11b Pigeon Pose Level 2, 5.11c Pigeon Pose Level 3

5.12a Kneeling Inner Thigh/Hip Flexor Stretch Level 1, 5.12b Kneeling Inner Thigh/Hip Flexor Stretch Level 2

5.13 Runner's Lunge

5.14 Plank Pose

5.15 Thigh Stretch

5.16 Side Bend

5.17 Reclining Hamstring Stretch

5.18 Reclining Inner Thigh Stretch

5.19 Reclining Outer Thigh Stretch

5.20a Passive Stretch, 5.20b Side Waists Stretch, 5.20c Shoulder Alignment Stretch

5.21a Seated Hero's Pose, 5.21b Seated Hero's Pose with Overhead Arm Stretch

5.22 Seated Hero's Pose with Handclasp Shoulder Stretch

5.23 Shoulder Blade Stretch

5.24 Waterfall

5.25 Ending Pose

Six

In the Office and on the Go

The two main things that lawyers do constantly all day—sit and deal with countless demands—are the very things that typically wreak the most havoc in their bodies. You wouldn't think that such normal stuff could be bad for you. Add the typical office experiences of the phone ringing off the hook, deadlines looming, the boss or clients breathing down your neck, a mounting workload, drowning in emails, eating at your desk. All the while speed up trying to catch up, and maybe a lot of time passes and not a lot gets done. Sedentary and overworked, many attorneys are stressed to the max and not functioning at peak performance.

Additionally, non-stop stress over time can lead to burn out, and according to statistics burnout in the legal profession is greater than that of other professions. This chapter explains the science of why working like this can lead to disturbing physiological results for so many. By understanding brain and body functioning and the stress response, we can alter the adverse physiological effects of work by modifying our behaviors and learning to work smarter.

This chapter focuses on work trends that utilize the emerging mind-body sciences to pioneer smarter ways to be more productive and avoid burnout. When you recharge yourself through mind-body techniques, minutes at a time throughout your day, you relax your nervous system, physically re-energize yourself, and invigorate the learning centers in your brain making you sharper and more able to be on task while providing a buffer against the occupational hazards of stress, depression, or burnout. Many of the mind-body exercises can be done at your desk or in your office, and some are inconspicuous enough to do at the airport, in a hallway, at the courthouse, or during a meeting. Taking mini "time off work" mind-body breaks also helps let go of tension before it turns to stress and helps let go of stress before it leads to burnout.

NON-STOP SITTING—THE HIGH COST OF A SEDENTARY LIFE

You've probably heard that sitting is hazardous to your health. Sitting is, for the most part, the primary "non-activity" lawyers engage in all day long. Long term it builds up fat stores contributing to weight gain (after an hour of sitting, production of enzymes that burn fat decline by 90 percent), it leads to chronic disease, and generally cuts years off your life. Here's why: Sitting triggers a harmful physiological response. It slows your body's metabolic rate, triggering a sort of hibernation mode. Your body cuts back all but the most critical systems—including your body's immune system—to bare minimum, letting much of you atrophy and decay. You simply deteriorate.

With non-stop sitting your chemistry becomes depressive. Maybe you just feel plain crummy, or gloomy, or foggy; perhaps your digestion's off; maybe your mind drifts. Your overall energy levels drop and you feel run down and tired at the end of the day because of being sedentary. You've entered a biological low-grade depression. The more you sit the less your body wants to move. And to not move is a depressant.

Besides the worrisome long-term effects, those hours spent sitting in front of your computer can affect your immediate life due to sitting in contorted, crippling posture and standing in slouchy positions that wreck your body. Do you experience sore joints, lousy balance, tightness and pain in the back, hips, shoulders, and neck? Is your breathing anxious and shallow?

How much worse can it get? If all this body news is not enough to get you up and moving, here's some other news for your brain. When chronic stress chemicals are combined with the biochemistry of not exercising, you get a chemical bath of inflammation. Inflammation wreaks mayhem in the body and brain, even contributing to plaque in the arteries of the brain, which could lead to stroke and dementia.

The good news is that movement and exercise counteract the effects of sitting. The other news is that going to the gym after work may not be enough. Research has suggested that a regular fitness regimen may be insufficient to counteract the effects of being sedentary during the day due to the adverse metabolic impact of sitting.

What do you do? The emerging research suggests you can sit without concern as long as you regularly interrupt your sitting with a few minutes of light or moderate activity. More on that later.

NON-STOP DEMANDS—THE HIGH COST OF CHRONIC STRESS

In the world of legal practice, non-stop demands produce stress. It happens all day long. Attorneys get used to it. It's normal. It comes with the territory.

Stress in and of itself is not necessarily the problem. In the 21st century, stress is part of being alive. There is such a thing as stress hardiness, that the right amount of stress can make us perform at higher levels, pushing us beyond the comfort zone and inspiring us to exceed limits.

But what's the right amount of stress, and how do you turn it off when you don't need it or want it? That's the real issue, because stress can easily become chronic. And we may not even realize we are living in chronic stress mode because we've forgotten what it feels like to feel really good. The long-term physical effects of stress are well documented. According to the American Medical Association, stress is a factor in more than 75 percent of all sickness. Additionally, when cortisol, one of the stress hormones, circulates in the body continuously for too long, it turns into a poison and eats holes in the hippocampus, which is the seat of memory in the brain. It severely weakens the immune system by interfering with normal T-cell production; this is linked to a range of illnesses, including diabetes and heart disease. Mind-body techniques can dial down or turn off the stress response so it does not become chronic. Physically, you feel better and your body functions better, preventing illness.

Stress affects us psychologically, as well. Many people who operate mostly "in their heads," like a lot of attorneys do, may be out of touch with the mind-body connection. Without the awareness the mind-body connection gives you, you can easily get derailed by your primitive brain and its cascade of stress chemistry before you realize what's happening. For lawyers, the intellect is supposed to be in charge. But the primitive brain is hard-wired to treat demands or deadlines and other psychological threats like life and death situations. Stress chemicals flood the body, preparing it to fight, freeze, or flee. With stress hormones coursing through you, you may lose the capacity to calmly think through ideal scenarios or take into account the long-range consequences of your actions. You may become exhausted, and therefore less productive, or maybe feel foggy or glum, overwhelmed or anxious. You may experience irritability, impatience, anxiety, or frustration, sometimes several times daily. Instead of being a rational counselor at law, you may have knee jerk reactions or emotional outbursts when the primitive brain is in charge. And once stress reaches critical, even the smallest setback triggers emotional hijack.

Mind-body techniques can produce awareness that allows for recognizing what you are feeling (your heart beating faster, a tightness in your chest, or any other signals you are going into stress mode) so you can consciously choose to defuse or neutralize negative emotions. With self-awareness and mind-body techniques, you can ward off reactivity and reclaim control.

Thus, it boils down to the lack of recovery from stress that gets us in trouble. We can easily get overly stressed and chronically stressed, unless we recharge with feel-good brain chemicals that produce positive emotions, counteract stress chemistry, build emotional resilience, and turn on the learning centers in the brain. These feel-good chemicals (dopamine, serotonin, and endorphins) can easily be accessed through the practice of mind-body techniques.

Stress happens all day long. When the stress response takes over it's not conscious, it's biological, and when chronic it can lead to disaster. We need ways during the day to turn off the stress response.

SMART WORK TRENDS

An alternative to sitting most of the day, nose to the grindstone, is a revolutionary way to feel better, think better, and perform better at work.

The explosion of research in the mind-body sciences makes the case for using mind-body techniques throughout the day. First, do the right things to relieve pain by sitting in good posture. Second, incorporate mini-breaks—intermittent recoveries of recharge—throughout the day.

The requirement for physical and psychological recharging is encoded in our biological makeup.

Two styles of recharge are offered in this chapter. Active recharge takes you out of hibernation mode and reinvigorates your body. Passive recharge switches off the stress response and turns on the stress antidotes of the feel-good brain-body chemicals. Both are useful throughout the day. Additionally, therapeutic yoga stretches help align your body so you can sit and stand in good posture. Good posture helps you get out of nagging pains, helps you breathe better, and helps you feel less stressed and more confident. Tips on how to sit well and stand well are presented in Chapter 3.

Using recharge techniques and stretches will help you feel more alert, have more energy, and be more efficient and productive. You notice almost immediately that you think more clearly and you feel more positive. Through recharging you build physical, mental, and emotional resilience as a buffer against physical decline, reactivity, depression, and burnout.

Carve out time to recharge. It's a priority that trumps everything. It could save your life.

TWO WAYS TO RECHARGE—ACTIVE RECHARGE AND PASSIVE RECHARGE

Recharging minutes at a time throughout your day will help you feel more alive, more connected to your body, more youthful, and optimistic. Use the two different ways to recharge when you need different results. For example, when you are drained from sitting, get active. When you are tired from not sleeping well the night before, do passive techniques for rest. When you are in pain or to prevent pain, stretch yourself. If you are edgy, out-of-sorts, and stressed, practice turning off the stress response with passive recharge. No matter which techniques you choose, when you are mindful of your breath, alignment, and body sensations you are "doing yoga" by connecting your mind, body, and breath. You are also practicing tools for better work-life balance and techniques to create a sense of well-being and equanimity that only the mind-body connection can give you.

ACTIVE RECHARGE

Thirty seconds, one minute, or up to five minutes at a time throughout your day helps prevent the body's hibernation response. It raises your heart rate and it's the simplest way to regenerate positive emotions after long hours of sitting. Movement and exercise energize and reinvigorate you. Most importantly it is an antidepressant, the magic talisman you possess to change yourself from apathetic, crippled, or exhausted. It perks you up. It's the master signaler that sets hundreds of chemical surges in motion that help you strengthen, grow, and repair.

EXERCISE 1: AEROBIC WAKE-UPS
The following mini bursts, for 30–60 seconds, can wake you up, tone you up, and get your blood flowing.

Standing:

Jumping jacks, jogging in place, marching your knees high, use the speakerphone and pace through your conversation, use the stairs.

Sitting:

March in your chair, pump your arms, lift your feet off the floor in a jogging motion to increase blood circulation in your lower body, with your arms out to sides shoulder level draw small circles in the air.

EXERCISE 2: CORE WAKE-UPS
Sit straight in your chair, grip the seat or armrests with your hands on either side of your thighs, engage your core and lift yourself up off the chair, hold for 10 seconds, lower yourself slowly. (Your feet

need not lift off the ground, as long as your core and your arms support your weight.) Repeat 3 times.

Standing with your hands and arms long by your sides, activate your core and gently rotate your torso and arms like a washing machine. Your heels lift off the ground as you move—this protects your joints. Your arms fly through space like empty coat sleeves and your fists tap gently at your hips.

EXERCISE 3: LOWER BODY WAKE-UP

Wall sits (Not for those with knee injuries)—Stand with your back in neutral touching a wall, feet shoulder-width apart. Bending at the hips and knees, walk your feet out until your thigh bones are parallel with the floor (don't go down so far if the knees are strained). Your shins are perpendicular to the floor, and your knees are directly above your heels. Use your core to lift weight out of the knees. Place your pelvis in neutral. Line up ears, shoulders, and hips in a neutral core-supported shape. Hold 30 seconds. Relax 5 seconds. Repeat for 5 minutes to crank up circulation in your legs and throughout your core.

(Alignment-wise this is great practice for how to sit well, as the wall behind your back gives you great feedback for keeping your pelvis and back neutral.)

EXERCISE 4: UPPER BODY WAKE-UPS

Wall push-ups—Stand well in good alignment, an arm's length away from a wall. Place your hands on the wall with straight arms, shoulder-width apart and at chest level. Bend your elbows out to the sides as your chest comes closer to the wall and your core-supported back stays neutral, and then push yourself back to straight arms. Repeat 15 times. Place hands armpit-wide at chest level and bend

elbows toward the ground feeling your triceps. Repeat 15 times. Place hands at chest level on the wall and make a triangle shape with your thumbs and index fingers. Bend elbows out to the sides. Repeat 15 times. Place your left hand on the wall at chest level and aim your fingers to the right. Place your right hand on the wall above your left and aim your fingers to the left. Bend elbows out to the sides. Repeat 15 times. Reverse hands and repeat 15 times.

EXERCISE 5: CHAIR PUSH-UPS

Strengthens the arms, wrists, shoulders, and core. Put the back of a chair against a wall. Place your hands on the chair seat walk your feet back until you are on the balls of your feet hip-width apart and your body is a neutral plank (use your core). Straighten the arms. To do pushups, bend your arms keeping your biceps facing the front and your triceps facing the back and your elbows close to

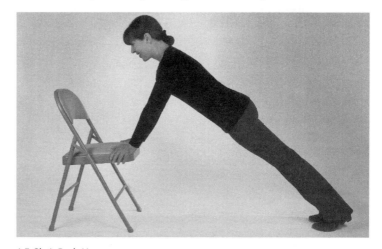

6.5 Chair Push-Ups

your ribs. Lower your chest staying neutral and using more core. Keep your shoulders away from your ears.

PASSIVE RECHARGE

This type of recharge soothes and relaxes your nervous system, and thereby lowers physiological arousal. The focus of your attention on your breath and body sensations helps you calm an over-active brain. The key is to unplug and completely change channels. Passive recharging requires full disengagement from work. It takes practice to learn how to do it, but once learned, it needn't take more than 2–10 minutes to kick in the "reset" button. When you become fully immersed in the sensations of your body you take a mental holiday, a vacation from stress. Your mind is engaged but relaxed. If you were to measure your brain waves on an EEG they would be similar to the state of meditation. You switch off the stress response, and the feel-good brain chemicals begin to flood your body. With practice recharging takes very little time to deeply quiet your mind and relax your body. Additionally, the seated and standing stretches are doable shapes designed to stretch your body into symmetry.

Use this breath exercise to prepare for passive recharge:

Sit with your back as straight and neutral as possible. With your hands on your thighs, close your eyes, relax your jaw, let your shoulders melt and your head float weightlessly. Imagining your torso as a giant balloon, inhale slowly allowing your breath to fill your side and back ribs and continue up into your chest and shoulders. Notice your side waists and spine get taller. Keep the length and exhale from your ribs then your chest, imagining tensions washing away. Repeat 3 times.

EXERCISE 6: YOGA FLOW

Stand. Do a shoulder roll front to back. Inhale as your arms float out to the sides and overhead, fingers reaching up, drawing a half circle up to the sky while your shoulders melt away from your ears. Stretch and breathe your side waists tall. Exhale and press your arms and palms back down as you soften and melt your shoulders. Keep a soft gaze, and a soft jaw. Repeat 5 times. If desired add a forward bend: on the inhale lift your arms out to the sides and overhead, using your core, exhale and dive forward hinging at the hips in neutral, arms out to the sides, and then hang in a forward bend (knees can be bent) with a hollow belly to lengthen your spine. Let your head go. Give it a shake, a nod, rock gently side to side. To come up: with bent knees press your hands into your thighs and use your core.

EXERCISE 7: SHOULDER SERIES

Push away from your desk. Sit at the front of your chair, feet hip-width and parallel, with your hands on your thighs. Inhale to elongate your trunk and broaden your chest.

Keep tall, inhale and lift your shoulders to your ears. Exhale as you roll your shoulders back and down.

Clasp your hands together. Turn your palms away. Press forward with your hands directly out from your chest straightening your arms as you bring your chin towards your chest, doming your upper back. Return your trunk to neutral.

Clasp your hands together. Turn your palms away. Press forward with your hands directly out from your chest. Straighten your arms and reach your palms up overhead, lift your chest, and arch your upper back. Return to neutral. Open your hands and release your arms down to your sides.

SEATED STRETCHES

Alleviates tension in the hands and forearms from spending hours at the computer.

EXERCISE 8: ANKLE TO KNEE HIP STRETCH

Do this stretch at intervals throughout the day and especially when the desire hits to "cross your legs." Cross one ankle over the opposite thigh letting the knee drop to the side. Flex your foot and align your ankle, and hinge forward from at the hips to a diagonal with a neutral back.

EXERCISE 9: SEATED TRICEPS STRETCH

Excellent for those with rounded shoulders, collapsed chests, or tight arms.

Sit with your back in neutral. Reach your left arm overhead. Turn your palm to face the wall behind you. Bend your left elbow and place your left fingers on your left shoulder. Your left elbow aims directly to the ceiling. Keep your torso neutral and core-supported and use your right hand over your head, fingers on your left elbow, to help lengthen the left triceps muscle and aim it flat toward the wall in front of you. Keep your back square, your shoulders level, and your collarbones broad and squared to the front. Lengthen your side waists and left armpit. Relax the entire left side of your body and breathe length into your left side. Release and switch sides.

6.8 Ankle to Knee Hip Stretch

6.9 Seated Triceps Stretch

EXERCISE 10: SEATED FRONT CHEST STRETCH

Stretches the chest, strengthens the upper back, and adds mobility to the shoulder girdle.

Sit with your back in neutral. Place your hands behind you, palms to rest at your pelvis. Point your fingers down. Inhale to lift your sternum bone. Keep your chest lifted and draw your shoulder blades and bent elbows slightly toward each other. Keeping your hands behind you, interlace your fingers pressing your knuckles toward the floor. Stay neutral as you straighten your arms behind you and roll your shoulders back and down. Inflate your lungs high into the chest and feel your collarbone widen.

EXERCISE 11: CHAIR LOW BACK STRETCH

Releases the low back and hips, massages the abdominal organs, and calms the nervous system.

Separate your legs so they are wider than hip-width. From your hip crease lengthen your side waists long, and then fold forward allowing your entire body to relax between your wide and parallel knees and feet. Allow your body, especially your neck and head, to completely hang in a relaxed rag doll manner. Hold your elbows or rest your hands on the floor.

6.10 Seated Front Chest Stretch

6.11 Chair Low Back Stretch

POWER POSES

Try these "power poses."

Using alignment, core support, right effort, and breath, power poses increase testosterone and decrease cortisol providing feelings of empowerment and increased confidence.

EXERCISE 13: SIDE ANGLE

EXERCISE 12: WARRIOR

6.12 Warrior

6.13 Side Angle

EXERCISE 14: STANDING HIP CREASE STRETCH WITH A CHAIR

Stretches the hips and inner groins.

Place the back of a chair against a wall. Stand three feet from the chair. Transfer your weight to your left foot and lift your right leg placing the ball of your foot on the edge of the chair. Keep your hips level. Bend your right knee, bring your pubic bone forward and soften your hip crease. Keep your back leg straight and use your core to keep your spine supported and lengthening. (You can put your hands on your hips.) Release and switch sides.

EXERCISE 15: LEG TO THE FRONT ON A CHAIR

Stretches the hamstrings and activates the core.

Place the back of a chair against a wall. Stand in neutral about a leg's length away from the seat of the chair. Use your core for support and balance. Lift your right leg and place your heel directly in front of you on the seat. Keep your hips level and your thighs active. As your flexibility increases practice with your leg on a higher prop, maybe the back of the chair. For further stretch in your side waists stretch your arms overhead with your palms facing each other. Release and switch sides.

6.14 Standing Hip Crease Stretch with a Chair

6.15 Leg to the Front on a Chair

EXERCISE 16: LEG TO THE SIDE ON A CHAIR

Stretches the hamstrings and activates the core.

Place the back of a chair against a wall. Stand in neutral sideways from the chair, leg distance away. Use your core for support and balance. Lift your right foot onto the chair and place your heel on the chair. Straighten this leg and make sure your knee faces the ceiling. Keep both legs active and the kneecaps lifted. Keep your hips and shoulders level. As your flexibility increases practice with your leg on a higher prop. Release and switch sides.

EXERCISE 17: STANDING THIGH STRETCH

Stretches the thigh and activates the core.

Rest your hand on a chair for support. Transfer your weight to your right foot and bend your left leg taking hold of the outside of your left aligned ankle with your left hand. Core-supported and neutral, slightly move your pelvis forward in space as you simultaneously draw your left knee directly back (not out to the side). Lift your hamstring muscles your sitting bones and lengthen your thigh. Release and switch sides.

6.16 Leg to the Side on a Chair

6.17 Standing Thigh Stretch

EXERCISE 18: UP DOG WITH A CHAIR

Strengthens the arms, stretches the chest, shoulders, belly, and sides, and activates the core.

Place the back of a chair against a wall. Place your hands on the chair seat. Walk your feet back about 3 to 4 feet from the chair. From a plank position move your pubic bone toward the chair and lengthen your spine vertically in a core-supported, even arc, keeping your legs strong. Keep your arms as vertical as possible and your shoulder tops away from your ears. Focus on the upward movement of your torso as you use the strength of your arms and the press of your hands. Glide the tips of your shoulder blades toward each other and broaden your collarbones. Continue to draw your low belly core in and lengthen your tailbone to support your low back. Look forward keeping your gaze soft and throat relaxed as you stretch out through the crown of your head.

6.18 Up Dog with a Chair

EXERCISE 19: GATE WITH A CHAIR

Stretches the sides and activates the core.

Place the back of a chair against a wall. With your standing leg about 3 to 4 feet away from the chair, bend your right knee and put your right foot, toes facing the wall, on the chair seat. Using your core, side bend to the right. Rest your right elbow on your thigh and lift your left arm overhead (keeping your shoulder blades flat on your back) to make the shape of a lateral C-curve as though your body is between two panes of glass. Melt your shoulders away from your ears. Breathe to lengthen your left side waist out of your pelvis. Release and switch sides.

6.19 Gate with a Chair

EXERCISE 20: DOWN DOG WITH A CHAIR

Stretches the entire back of the body, opens the chest, and improves breathing.

Place the back of a chair against a wall. Place your hands on the chair. Hinge at your hips, walking your feet back until your hips are over your ankles. Your core is supporting your neutral-back. Work on straightening your arms and legs, but if needed, you can slightly bend your knees. Elongate from your head to your tail reaching through your arms. Feel your side waists and spine lengthen. Slide your shoulders away from your ears.

EXERCISE 21: STANDING FORWARD BEND ON A CHAIR

Stretches the back, softens the hip crease, activates the core.

Stand with your feet hip-width apart and your right side touching the chair seat. Lift your right leg and place your foot in parallel on the chair seat bending the knee. Make sure your right foot is aligned with your left, which is about 12 inches from the chair seat. Lift the kneecap of the standing leg. From the hip crease lean forward rounding your back into a cat-back shape supported by your core. You can let go in the pose by clasping your elbows, dropping your head, and relaxing your neck. Breathe deeply into your back. Release and switch sides. ❈

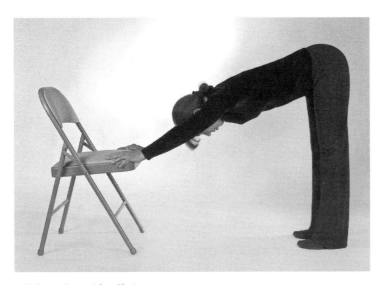

6.20 Down Dog with a Chair

6.21 Standing Forward Bend on a Chair

6.5 Chair Push-Ups

6.8 Ankle to Knee Hip Stretch

6.9 Seated Triceps Stretch

6.10 Seated Front Chest Stretch

6.11 Chair Low Back Stretch

6.12 Warrior

6.13 Side Angle

6.14 Standing Hip Crease Stretch

6.15 Leg to the Front on a Chair

6.16 Leg to the Side on a Chair

6.17 Standing Thigh Stretch

6.18 Up Dog with a Chair

6.19 Gate with a Chair

6.20 Down Dog with a Chair

6.21 Standing Forward Bend on a Chair

Seven

Dead Tired: Restorative Yoga to De-Stress and Recharge

Relaxation is the ultimate antidote to stress. There is a skill and an art to it, and restorative yoga is an ideal way to learn it. Relaxation is a gradual process. It takes practice. It's a state of mind in which you are so utterly at ease that there is no external body movement and the brain is noise-free.

When you practice mini-breaks of restorative yoga throughout your day or after work, your nervous system learns to let go of physical and emotional tensions. Minutes a day help to heal the effects of chronic stress and add to your energy. Regular practice releases muscular tension and headaches, reduces fatigue, improves sleep, and enhances immune system function.

Restorative yoga boosts the "rest and repair" response of the parasympathetic nervous system. The "fight or flight" sympathetic nervous system is calmed. When practicing restorative yoga, your heartbeat slows, your respiration steadies, and your respiratory capacity increases allowing your brain to use oxygen more efficiently. Your blood pressure lowers, levels of stress hormones decrease, and your body's healing mechanisms are turned on.

INTRODUCTION TO RESTORATIVE YOGA

Restorative yoga is the easiest way to turn off the stress chemistry and turn on the "good feeling" brain chemicals, dopamine and serotonin. As you learn to relax in restorative yoga, you'll also feel the benefits in your daily life. You'll automatically be able to conserve your energy instead of feeling like you are running on empty. You'll automatically become more efficient and clear thinking.

Restorative yoga uses a variety of props—blankets, bolsters, foam rollers, straps, blocks, chairs, and the wall. There is no need to buy anything. To find props around your house or office, think creatively—sofa cushions, blankets, chairs, soft belts, bathrobe ties, or neckties.

Props provide for deeper relaxation. They allow you to stay in the pose for longer periods of time. Sometimes it takes two or three minutes just to settle into a pose with real and deep relaxation coming only after that settling period. Props also teach proper architecture of the pose and educate your body to align itself correctly. Restorative yoga is designed to use very little muscular effort because of the props that support you. It's a way to have deep rest whenever you want it, and it's the best way to recharge your energy. It's more restful than taking a nap because even during sleep your mind is still active and your body may toss and turn.

Stress causes over-stimulation of your nervous system and that causes inability to relax your body and mind. You may feel agitated. Agitation and resultant muscular tension may cause insomnia. When you are sleep deprived you are more unbalanced with greater vulnerability to stress. You try to cope and end up burning the candle at both ends. During the day you are groggy and inefficient. During the night you are tense and worried about everything, including not being able to sleep. So begins a vicious cycle.

Sleep science tells us to sleep seven to eight hours of good sleep each night. Sleep science tells us sleep is important for memory. Skills learned during the day are then refined in sleep. The brain sifts through information and makes sense of the day in a way that can only happen in sleep. Sleep also wards off major health concerns and is the foundation of physical energy.

Restorative yoga directly affects sleep. In fact, people often report sleeping much better after practicing restorative yoga. As you learn to relax your body, you will also learn to relax your mind. Restorative yoga teaches you ways to prevent being swept away by thoughts and emotions, which is an important skill to master, especially if you are being kept awake by ruminations on the past, future, or "what ifs."

Restorative yoga teaches mind-body connecting skills. Breath exercises and breath instructions as well as the use of your imagination and visualizations help your brain learn to let go of incessant mental chatter that may keep you on edge. When you relax your head and face, your body follows. When you relax your body, your mind follows. When you notice these things happening, you are automatically learning and internalizing the mind-body connection.

When you register the body sensations inherent in "letting go" into states of relaxation, you are training your mind-body connection. When you breathe deeply through your nose in a long and slow rhythm and notice places of tension and relaxation in your body, you are automatically connecting your mind to your body and to the present moment. Being present means observing and responding appropriately.

When you learn to do this in restorative yoga you are also teaching yourself how to rationally observe and appropriately respond in daily life, even under stressful conditions. When you scan your body from head to toe, noticing tensions and letting them go, you are using your mind-body connection. The mind-body connection gives you entrance to your inner environment. By reducing input coming into your senses (eyes, ears, mouth, nose), you allow yourself to observe, feel, and listen to what's taking place inside the body. There is a soothing effect on your nervous system.

You start to notice a rise and fall of your abdomen with your breath, your heart beating slowly and regularly, perhaps your belly gurgling, or your mind jumping. As the restorative yoga props relieve your bones and muscles of their role of support, your nervous system sends fewer messages and your body and mind become quieter as layers of tension melt away. You replace over-stimulation with relaxation and quietude. The focus of your attention on your breath helps you calm any churning of your thinking brain as you learn to focus on your body sensations. When you become fully immersed in the sensations of your body, you take a mental holiday, a vacation from stress. You turn off the spigot of the stress response and the feel-good brain chemicals begin to flood your body.

> Having a strong mind-body connection is critical to rational thinking. The mind-body connection teaches your nervous system to face difficult situations with greater ease. You become more resilient.

GENERAL GUIDELINES FOR PRACTICING RESTORATIVE YOGA

If you have heart disease or hypertension that is not controlled by medication, keep your head above your heart and don't elevate your legs above your heart.

Whenever possible, breathe in and out through your nose—this air is filtered and warmed, and this allows relaxation of your head and jaw. Breathing is always slow and steady and without force.

Learn to let go fully, releasing tensions through the mind-body connection. You will be better able to notice body and breath sensations with your eyes relaxed and closed.

If you experience pain in a pose, come out of the pose and rearrange your props. Alternatively, back out of the pose, and modify it by asking yourself what muscles you can relax to have the pain disappear, what additional props you can add, or what better alignment you can create so as to not feel pain. Make sure that when you are resting in a pose, you are pain-free.

Stretching too aggressively in a pose can lead to strain. Practice yielding rather than forcing or straining.

Move in slow motion in and out of a pose. Moving abruptly destroys the calming effect and may strain a muscle.

After you come out of a pose, sit in neutral to let all your muscles regroup in a natural position.

Always check for tension in your neck and jaw and align your neck.

When you lie on your back, position your chin level with your forehead or slightly lower than your forehead to calm the frontal lobes of the brain. Be sure to not flatten your neck spine but allow its natural relaxed curve, supported with the correct height of props.

Pay special attention to the comfort of your low back and proceed cautiously if you have chronic back pain.

In each pose, a good rule of thumb is to spend 10–20 slow, steady breaths in the pose and stay no more than 5–6 minutes unless you are in the "Peaceful" or "Deep Relaxation" poses.

Use any of the breathing instructions found in the luxurious relaxation poses for any other restorative yoga posture, or be creative with your breath, sending it to different parts of your body while noticing the effects.

FIVE CATEGORIES OF POSES

This chapter describes five categories of restorative yoga: Luxurious Relaxation; Better Back Relaxation; Better Shoulders Relaxation; Better Immune System; and Breath Exercise.

LUXURIOUS RELAXATION POSES

This section explains Simple Relaxation Pose, Supported Bound Angle Rest, Supported Waterfall, Supported Reclining Twist, Supported Child's Pose.

EXERCISE 1: SIMPLE RELAXATION POSE

Props needed: a strap and a pillow if desired.

This pose, along with the breathing instructions below, teaches skills to calm your mind and turn off the stress response. The skills learned here including the yogic breathing can be used in all the restorative poses.

Remember to follow these general guidelines for this pose and all the other poses as well.

Breathe in and out through your nose, keep your eyes relaxed and closed, align your neck by positioning and supporting your head with a blanket or pillow if needed so that your chin is level with your forehead or slightly lower than your forehead.

7.1 Simple Relaxation Pose

Observe the position of your body. Arrange your arms and legs equidistant from your midline. You can place a strap around your thighs if it helps hold your legs. The idea is to not use any muscles when you are in the pose. Place your feet apart and let your knees fall toward each other. Slightly lift your pelvis so you can use your hands to ease the flesh of your buttocks away from your head, lengthening your low back, and then place your pelvis back on the ground. The position of your legs broadens your low back muscles. Feel your low back and entire spine heavy and at ease. Your belly should be soft. Imagine the skin of your face heavy as it drapes over the bones of your face. Allow your forehead, cheekbones, and brow bone to feel heavy as well. Imagine that your eyes recede, your eyelids soften and melt, the back of your tongue relaxes and melts away from the roof of mouth, and your jaw releases. Feel your bones heavy, your muscles drop, your skin loose and heavy.

Initially your breath spreads your ribs wide on your inhale. At the fullest point in your inhale, pause before melting into a long, slow, steady exhale. Exhale fading into an imaginary vast open space like the night sky. Pause briefly at the end of your exhale. Once you find a slow sideways ribcage breath (approximately six counts to fill and six or seven counts or more to empty), expand your breath into your back ribs as well. When you've found this full ribcage breath, let your breath travel even further upward as you inhale all the way up to your top chest and top shoulders—the full yogic breath. Side, back, and all the way up goes the inhale (six counts or so) and the exhale releases tensions like leaves washing downstream (over six or seven or more slow steady counts).

Continue this full yogic breath and observe how your inhale informs you of tight places in your body, and how the exhale lets go of the tensions. Absorbed in the present moment, you are your breath and your breath is you. Give your full attention to breathing while you observe body sensations that become more pronounced as you breathe and relax.

EXERCISE 2: SUPPORTED BOUND ANGLE REST

Props needed: three to four long-folded blankets or a bolster, two blocks, a strap.

This pose relaxes your abdomen and physically frees up the main areas of your body that are typically tight and restricted by sitting—your chest and your entire pelvis. The pose also passively stretches your inner thighs and hips. You may experience a feeling of floating.

Sit on the ground directly in front of the short end of the stacked blankets or a bolster with your prop touching your tail-bone. Use a blanket or pillow under your head so that it's higher than your heart and your chin is level with your forehead. Bring the soles of your feet together with your heels a foot away from you and let your knees fall out to the sides. Now prop your outer thighs up with blocks so the stretch is not too intense. At your back, place a wide looped strap below your waist around your pelvic bones and feet. As you recline, use your hands to ease the flesh of your buttocks away from your head, lengthening your low back.

Practice three-part breathing while in the pose. Initially do several rounds of belly breathing (on the inhale the belly and low back gently push away from the spine). Then progress to several rounds of chest breathing (on the inhale the front and back ribs expand). Finally, complete several rounds of top lung breathing (on the inhale the chest lifts, the collar bones widen, and you feel the breath in the back and top shoulders).

7.2 Supported Bound Angle Rest

EXERCISE 3: SUPPORTED WATERFALL

Props needed: three to four long-folded blankets or a bolster.

This pose relaxes your abdomen, aids in digestion, and physically frees up the main areas of your body that are typically tight and restricted from sitting—your chest and your entire pelvis. It also creates a gentle traction in your low back.

In this pose, your head is higher than your chest and your chest is higher than your pelvis. Sit on the ground directly in front of the short end of the stacked blankets or bolster, with your prop touching your tailbone. Place an extra blanket or pillow under your head so it's higher than your heart and your chin is level with your forehead. As you recline, use your hands to ease the flesh of your buttocks away from you, lengthening your low back.

Imagine you are tracing the natural curves of your spine with your breath. As you inhale, imagine your breath drawing a line up the front of your spine from bottom to top. On your exhale, imagine the breath drawing a line down the back of your spine from top to bottom.

Before you exit the pose, you may want to lift your arms to the ceiling and then overhead to give yourself a long stretch through your side waists. Alternatively, you can hold the crooks of your elbows with your hands, lengthening your trunk.

EXERCISE 4: SUPPORTED RECLINING TWIST

Props needed: three to four stacked long-folded blankets or a bolster.

This pose relieves back tension, lengthens back and side muscles, stretches intercostal muscles between the ribs, and enhances breathing.

Sit next to the prop with your right hip next to the short end of the bolster, and your knees bent and feet to the side of your left hip. Turn toward the bolster and rest your torso face down.

7.3 Supported Waterfall

7.4a Supported Reclining Twist

Place your arms in a comfortable position and rest your right cheek on the bolster. For a slightly deeper twist rearrange your torso to comfortably place your left cheek on the bolster. Repeat on the opposite side.

Practice breathing into your ribcage, further stretching your rib muscles with your breath.

EXERCISE 5: SUPPORTED CHILD'S POSE

Props needed: three to four long-folded blankets or a bolster.

This pose stretches, relieves, and soothes the low back and shoulders. It is also emotionally comforting.

Kneel on the floor with your knees apart. Use padding on the floor for your shins if needed. Sit on your heels and put the bolster or stacked blankets between your thighs. Make a high enough stack so when you fold forward with a deep hip crease, you can relax onto the support without holding yourself up at all. Fold your torso over onto the prop, resting your head to one side. Half way through the hold turn your head. Ideally your spine will round evenly while your chest rests on the bolster and your tailbone drops toward your heels, lengthening your low back.

Your buttocks do not have to touch your heels. Find a comfortable position for your arms. Periodically lift your torso slightly, elongate your spine, and drape your body further forward.

If you experience discomfort in your knees, ankles, or tops of your feet, put a folded towel into the bend of your knees, and a rolled towel under the front of your ankles, letting your feet hang over the roll.

Try back breathing. Feel your inhale "puff" your whole back, filling it like a balloon.

7.4b Supported Reclining Twist

7.5 Supported Child's Pose

POSES FOR BETTER BACK RELAXATION

This section explains Cross-legged Forward Bend, Pigeon at the Wall, Bound Angle at the Wall, Knee Hug, Straps around Feet, Child's Pose.

EXERCISE 6: CROSS-LEGGED FORWARD BEND

Props needed: none.

This pose stretches out the outer thighs and hips and lengthens the side waists.

Begin by sitting in a simple cross-leg position. Keep your sitting bones in contact with the floor, acting as an anchor. From this base, lean forward at a diagonal, placing your hands on the floor in front of your legs. Lengthen the sides of your torso from your hips to your armpits. Creep your hands further forward as you round your back, dropping your forehead down toward the floor. Let your front ribs come to lie on your legs. Next, walk your hands to lengthen your side waists and spine at a diagonal, inside your thigh. Repeat on the other side.

7.6a Cross-Legged Forward Bend

7.6b Cross-Legged Forward Bend

EXERCISE 7: PIGEON AT THE WALL

Props needed: the wall.

This pose stretches the outer thighs and hips.

Begin by lying on your back far enough away from the wall so you can place your feet flat on the wall with your legs forming a right angle. Create a straight line with your spine. Place the sole of your left foot on the wall and cross your right ankle over your left thigh just below the left knee. Flex your right foot and ease your knee away from you, keeping the midline of your spine and keeping your pelvis level. Repeat on the other side.

EXERCISE 8: BOUND ANGLE AT THE WALL

Props needed: the wall.

This pose creates ideal spinal alignment.

Begin by lying on your back the right distance from a wall. Create a straight line with your spine. Bring the soles of your feet together bending your knees out to the sides. Gently lengthen your inner thighs.

7.7 Pigeon at the Wall

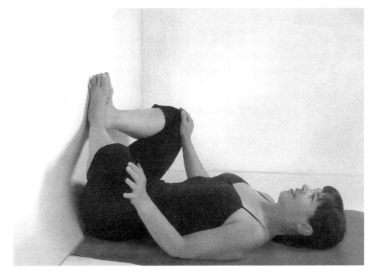

7.8 Bound Angle at the Wall

EXERCISE 9: KNEE HUG

Props needed: none.

This pose releases the spine, resets the low back, and helps realign the pelvis which may have tight leg and back muscles from poor posture.

Lie on your back in neutral hugging your knees into your chest. Add the motion of "stirring" your thigh bones in your hip sockets.

EXERCISE 10: STRAPS AROUND FEET

Props needed: two straps.

This pose helps you isolate the hip sockets, relax the low back, lengthen the side waists, and soften the front hip creases.

Keep your spine elongated and your back in neutral resting on the floor as you fold your thighs toward your armpits, and position your feet over your knees. Use as much strap length as necessary to allow the spine and shoulders to be at ease with your arms deep into the sockets.

EXERCISE 11: CHILD'S POSE

Props needed: a blanket (optional).

This pose broadens and relaxes the back, lengthens and decompresses the spine, and softens the hip flexors.

Sit on your heels and fold forward over your thighs. Your torso should remain in contact with your thighs, and your sitting bones should remain in contact with your heels. Gently touch your forehead on the floor or on a folded blanket to rest the brain's frontal lobe. Make sure your arms are comfortable. Your back should round evenly. Experiment with taking your knees closer together or farther apart. If the buttocks stay high in the air and you feel as if you are nosediving, add one or more blankets to prop your forehead higher.

7.9 Knee Hug

7.10 Straps Around Feet

7.11 Child's Pose

POSES FOR BETTER SHOULDER RELAXATION

This section explains Ideal Posture Backbend, Wall Hang with Shoulder Stretch, Resting Dog

EXERCISE 12: IDEAL POSTURE BACKBEND

Props needed: two blocks

This pose helps create better posture by training the upper chest muscles to roll over the top shoulders and down the back.

Place two blocks at different heights. Ideally the shoulder block is placed at the first height and the head block is placed at the second height.

Lift your chest bone (sternum) up as you recline onto the shoulder block, placing the bottom of your shoulder blades on one block and your head on the tallest block. Stretch your legs straight or bend your knees with the soles of the feet on the floor. Use your hands to smooth the skin of the buttocks away from your head, lengthening your low back. Let your arms rest at your sides, palms up. Your top shoulder bones melt with gravity toward the ground, passively pulling width across the collar bones as the skin of the chest passively moves up over the top shoulders and down the back, while the neck lengthens in its relaxed natural curve.

EXERCISE 13: WALL HANG WITH SHOULDER STRETCH

Props needed: the wall.

This pose lengthens your trunk and turns your senses inward. It also stretches the muscles of the shoulders and arms.

Stand far enough away from a wall so that you won't nosedive as you bend forward. Place your feet hip-width apart in parallel, and place your pelvis against the wall. Bend your knees, fold-

7.12 Ideal Posture Backbend

7.13 Wall Hang with Shoulder Stretch

ing your upper body so your torso is elongated. Hinging at your hips with your knees bent, touch the floor, or for higher support, touch the seat of a chair with your hands. Be sure the chair will not slide away from you. Hollow your belly and slowly start to straighten your legs, sliding your sitting bones up the wall any amount. Lengthen your arms and relax your shoulders away from your ears, using your arms and hands to press your pelvis into the wall. Avoid collapsing into your shoulder joints by maintaining a neutral torso. Notice your spine and side waists elongate. Fully relax your neck and face.

EXERCISE 14: RESTING DOG
Props needed: one block.

This pose supports the head to calm the mind and relax the nervous system, all while allowing the backs of the legs and the shoulders to stretch and the side waists and spine to elongate.

Kneel on all fours (table position), knees directly under hips. Keep your hands, knees, and feet hip-width apart. Place a block on the floor just below the chest.

Make sure your wrist creases are perpendicular to your torso and that your arms are straight. Curl your toes under, press into your flat palms, lift your knees, and rise into an inverted "V" position on your tiptoes with bent knees. Your ribs will come toward your thighs. Lengthen your side waists as your sitting bones lift.

Keep your torso core supported in neutral—avoid pushing your low ribs forward and collapsing into your shoulder joints. Keep your knees bent. This encourages non-rounding. Start to straighten your legs while maintaining the straight inverted "V" shape of your back. Your hips should stay high as your pelvis presses back in

7.14 Resting Dog

space toward your heels, forming a straight spine and a straight line from your hands to your hips. If it reaches, rest the weight of your head onto the tallest height of the block. This will allow your neck and facial muscles to relax completely.

BETTER IMMUNE SYSTEM POSES
This section explains Legs Up the Wall, Supported Bridge, Inverted Chair Rest, Deep Relaxation Pose.

Inversions reverse the effects of gravity, by reversing the flow of blood and lymph fluid that accumulates in the lower extremities. When fluids are returned to the upper body, heart function is enhanced and brain arousal is reduced.

EXERCISE 15: LEGS UP THE WALL

Props needed: the wall.

This pose reduces fatigue, enhances circulation, reduces swelling in the legs, and enhances the immune system.

Sit with your right side to the wall and recline on your side. Swing your legs up the wall while allowing your left shoulder to roll toward the ground at the same time as your legs are moving up the wall. Recline onto your back. Push yourself toward the wall so your hips are as close to the wall as possible with your whole back in neutral, flat and relaxed on the ground. Extend your legs up the wall. With the help of gravity, your sacrum will stay flat on the ground. Bend your knees slightly if that is more comfortable.

If you experience any strain in the back of your knees, move far enough away from the wall so you can bend your knees and rest the soles of your feet on the wall. Make sure your low back is not rounded and your tailbone and buttocks are not lifting off the floor. If they are, move away from the wall so your low back is comfortable and supported by the floor. If your chin lifts toward the ceiling, place a blanket under your head and neck to support the cervical curve in your back. Keep your chin slightly level with your forehead. When your position feels just right, look along your body to check that your trunk is perpendicular to the wall.

While in this pose, imagine your brain moving away from your forehead and sinking toward the back of the head.

7.15 Legs Up the Wall

EXERCISE 16: INVERTED CHAIR REST

Props needed: a chair, blankets.

This pose relaxes abdominals and low back, and reduces fatigue.

Place a blanket on the chair, with more blankets on the floor.

7.16 Inverted Chair Rest

Lie down on the floor, blankets close to the chair, and place your calves on the seat. Bend your legs to form right angles. Allow the blankets on the floor to support your low and middle back. Allow your shoulder blades to rest on floor. Allow your arms to rest alongside your body, palms up, and keep your chin level with your forehead. Allow your back to melt and sink. This takes all the weight and tension off the back. Allow the legs to feel as though they are levitating and scan your entire body for relaxation.

EXERCISE 17: DEEP RELAXATION POSE
Props needed: a blanket.

This pose creates deep relaxation as the name suggests. The "personal retreat" aspect described below is helpful to many lawyers to use daily at work, seated at their desks. When they notice a heavy dose of stress or an uncomfortable emotion coming on, they retreat for a couple of minutes (or sometimes even less than a minute) into their personal safe haven where they notice the stress evaporate. Then they are able to continue with whatever it was that had initially brought on the stress response in a clear and level-headed way.

In this neutral pose, the spine elongates with its natural curves and your midline and limbs are equidistant from your trunk. Your palms are up, and your shoulder blades are heavy with relaxation and flush against the floor. Your chin and forehead are at equal height. As you scan your body, bones, muscles, skin, and brain, cease fidgeting as you let go of tension.

Your legs are hip-width apart. If you like, you can cover yourself with a blanket. The tendency is to get cold as you drop into deeper brain waves. Release all unnecessary tension in your forehead, eyes, tongue, jaw, shoulders, arms, torso and legs. While your body lets go, your mind stays alert. As you take a break from external movement, allow your mind to become acutely sensitive to internal sensations. Notice a heightened awareness, and as thoughts roll in, bring your attention back to your body sensations.

You may simply rest here listening to relaxing music or practicing breathing exercises. Or, use this time to create your own personal retreat—think of a place where you know you can feel completely at ease. This can become a tool to help you feel relaxed and in control of your experiences in daily life, an internal safe haven. Create a multi-sensory image in your mind and feel it in your body. This becomes a place you can return to at any time when you need to feel at ease. The image can be of a real place you've been before or an imaginary place. The important thing is that

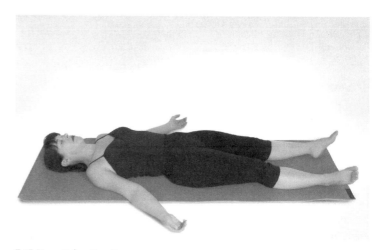

7.17 Deep Relaxation Pose

when you focus on this place, you feel at ease. You could see and feel yourself seated by a stream or a still pond, near an ocean, in a lush green forest, in a special room surrounded by your favorite things, being with a loved one, floating on a cloud, being in any special place you've been before or one that comes to you in your imagination. (Perhaps, additionally add conscious, slow, steady breathing while experiencing your personal retreat.)

Use your senses inside of your private retreat. Hear the call of birds or other sounds like leaves in the wind or a brook. Smell, taste, and feel. Allow images to come into your awareness. You can create and practice being in your retreat in deep relaxation pose so that it will be easy to retreat to this place in your daily life when you want to relax and feel at ease. You can also use your retreat if you have trouble falling asleep at night. It is also helpful to use if you feel extreme emotions coming on. The more aspects of imagination, sensory input (sounds, tastes, smells, sights), and body sensation that you can use to create and experience your retreat, the more effective a tool it will be.

BREATH EXERCISE

EXERCISE 18: BREATHING

Props needed: none.

This exercise relaxes the nervous system, helping you feel more centered and balanced physically, mentally, and emotionally.

There are two simple types of breathing: belly breathing and chest breathing. For belly breathing, on the inhale the belly gently pushes away from the spine, and on the exhale the belly comes in toward the spine. For chest breathing, on the inhale the ribs and chest expand, and on the exhale the ribs and chest relax.

Both types of breathing calm and relax the mind and are an effective mini break from stress. An easy way to practice in the beginning is to make a tape of these instructions and use the tape during lunch or mid-day breaks. This breathing will eventually become second nature. Use an optimal sitting position explained in Chapter 6.

The following is a balanced combination of belly breathing and chest breathing and nose breathing and mouth breathing. The breath is relaxed, slow and steady, and never forced. Practice five rounds of each kind of breath.

Chest Breath—inhale nose and exhale nose (5X)
Chest Breath—inhale nose and exhale mouth (5X)
Belly Breath—inhale mouth and exhale nose (5X)
Chest Breath—inhale left nostril and exhale right nostril (5X)
Chest Breath—inhale right nostril and exhale left nostril (5X)
Belly Breath—inhale nose and exhale nose (5X)
Belly Breath—inhale mouth and exhale mouth (5X)
Chest Breath—inhale in 5 parts through the nose like quick sniffing breaths and exhale through the mouth in 5 parts like quick blowing breaths (5X)✳

7.1 Simple Relaxation Pose

7.2 Supported Bound Angle Rest

7.3 Supported Waterfall

7.4a Supported Reclining Twist, 7.4b Supported Reclining Twist

7.5 Supported Child's Pose

7.6a Cross-Legged Forward Bend, 7.6b Cross-Legged Forward Bend

7.7 Pigeon at the Wall

7.8 Bound Angle at the Wall

7.9 Knee Hug

7.10 Straps Around Feet

7.11 Child's Pose

7.12 Ideal Posture Backbend

7.13 Wall Hang with Shoulder Stretch

7.14 Resting Dog

7.15 Legs Up the Wall

7.16 Inverted Chair Rest

7.17 Deep Relaxation Pose

8

Meditation and Other Ways to Calm the Mind

As attorneys, the brain is clearly our most useful organ, yet we don't always do enough to protect it from harm. As we've discussed, we often eat and drink too much, lack physical exercise, and probably most harmful of all, we don't give the brain a break. Ever. We work on the train, on the elevator, in the car on our way to and from work. We work while running and walking the dog. The truth is that at least some of these times, we could be resting and clearing the brain for better future thinking. As it turns out, cutting out the static and noise in the brain can have a transformative effect on your ability to effectively and efficiently practice law.

One thing emphasized in Jon Kabat-Zinn's book, *Full Catastrophe Living*,[44] is the deep connection between mind and body. Many meditation books focus only on the mind, missing the benefits of working with this vital connection. For lawyers, it is often necessary to work through the body in order to quiet the mind. We may be barely aware of our body most of the time and unaware of how it feels in general as well as in various individual parts.

Yet listening to our own bodies greatly improves health. Relaxation can remain elusive when we are storing tension in our shoulders, jaws, forehead, and hips. To release this tension, you need to know it is there. The body scan described in *Yoga Nidra* below helps

with this, as does all of the yoga in this book.

We can relax the body through yoga or, when that is not available, we can use our minds to slowly release the tension-intense areas and finally let go of it, relaxing into our own skin. This chapter explains how, and also explains how the mind-body connection can open up surprising possibilities in life.

MEDITATION CAN DEEPLY ENHANCE THE PRACTICE OF LAW

As we alluded to in all prior chapters, the mind works best when we clear it of debris now and then. Ironically, the only real way to clear the mind, improve creativity, and increase productivity is to clear out the cobwebs. You already have experienced this when searching for an answer to a perplexing and enduring problem. Answers remain elusive despite your hardest and deepest concentration and then, boom, it comes to you on a dog walk or in the shower.

The effects of meditation on the lawyer's mind are significant, as noted by Professor Charles Halpern. In his book, *Making Waves and Riding Currents*,[45] this former CUNY Law School Dean and Arnold and Porter attorney talks about the first time he ever experienced meditative moments, which occurred on a canoe in the lakes of northern Ontario. These experiences later led to a more formal meditation practice, which he claims altered his life and law practice in measurable positive ways. As he explains:

> I found that in the midst of turmoil I was able to respond to strong pressure with less anger and reactivity. I was able to see things more clearly. I was able to empathize with a broad range of people and identify the things we shared . . . .

> Each of us can return to times in our lives when we had an awakening—an insight that suggested that the world was larger than what we had thought it was. Often these are not the sort of incidents that show up on résumés, and we sometimes don't talk about them with the people we work with. By sharing such incidents in my life, I want to encourage each of us to lift up to such events, to reflect on how they enrich our lives, and how they can be more fully integrated into our work for a more peaceful and just world.[46]

Similarly, law professor Leonard Riskin has meditated for many decades and currently teaches dispute resolution and mindfulness in law at the University of Florida as well as Northwestern School of Law. He recounts the many benefits of meditation for lawyers in a groundbreaking 2002 law review article.[47] According to one Hale and Dorr attorney that Riskin quotes, meditation helps her:

- think through things and respond more effectively,
- manage stress better and not be so affected by it,
- be more tolerant and less judgmental,
- listen better,
- pay more attention to other people,
- get to know people better, and
- develop harmony between work-self and other-time-self.[48]

Another meditator that Professor Riskin quotes claims that meditation causes him to feel better, be more efficient, be less likely to jump to conclusions, and be more likely to see any issue from more angles, which is the key to solving legal problems.[49]

The legal world as a whole is starting to notice these benefits. In his book about using mindfulness in the practice of law, *Transforming Practices*, Steven Keeva outlines numerous meditation methods, describes many attorneys who use them, and describes the benefits.[50] He outlines how meditation can quiet the mind, improve empathy, boost energy, clarify thinking, and create a deep and sustained peace of mind.

THE SCIENCE BEHIND MEDITATION

Numerous scientific studies demonstrate the benefits of meditation on both emotional and cognitive heath. One well-regarded paper found that regular transcendental meditation benefitted the elderly in numerous measurable ways, by:

- increasing longevity,
- reducing blood pressure to healthy levels,
- improving mental health,
- increasing cognitive flexibility (evidenced by less premature cognitive commitment, increased learning ability on associa-

tive learning and greater perceptual flexibility, increasing word fluency, increasing the ability to cope with minor inconveniences, reduced feelings of being old, less impatience with others), and

- creating a greater overall sense of well-being.[51]

Many other studies have found similar results, leading some people to conclude that taking time to be mindful and clear the mind of debris can, generally speaking, make people better at virtually anything.[52] Meditation helps not just with concentration and problem-solving but also with improving sleep.

Perhaps these are the reasons why meditation has suddenly become so popular in law firms like Boston's Hale and Dorr, O'Melvany & Meyers (which incidentally has the URL of .OMM), as well as many, many others. It also may explain why meditation has found its way into so many law school classes.[53] The University of Miami has an entire mindfulness curriculum, which includes many forms of meditation as well as yoga.

KEEPING AN OPEN MIND ABOUT MEDITATION TECHNIQUES

There are many ways to think about meditation, but at its most fundamental, meditation clears the mind so you can think better. This allows you to remain focused and to complete tasks more thoughtfully and thoroughly, often in less time than they would otherwise take. There is no real way to welcome clearing and creatively solve a problem when the mind is filled with shopping lists, to-do lists, half-written legal briefs, scripts of difficult phone calls, etc.

To get started clearing the mind, try to put all that debris in writing and then free it from your mind. If you practice law, you already make lists but the purpose of this exercise is different. You are simply trying to release negative or repetitive thoughts by writing them down. Now you are ready to meditate.

Most people meditate to free the mind of chatter and clarify thinking. You do not need to free your mind of *all* thoughts in order for meditation to help you. While experienced meditators may be able to free the mind of thoughts for hours at a time, even a glimpse at a clear mind for a few seconds can show you the potential of meditation. Indeed, just slowing down thoughts during a brief meditation (10 to 15 minutes) can itself work wonders. Ultimately, if you were able to slow down the thought process by 50 percent for even a short time, you would think more clearly and feel a sense of deep relief.

When you meditate, whether in guided or unguided meditation, don't fight the thoughts that will inevitably arise. Just acknowledge the thoughts and then release them. This will help you slow down the thoughts and feel calmer.

Meditation sometimes creates another useful side effect. Sometimes some truth you have known about but have been avoiding bubbles up. By paying attention to what bubbles up, you can gain true self-awaress, grow and become happier and healthier in the long run

Keep an open mind about what counts as meditation. As Zen master Jon Kabat-Zinn notes in both his helpful beginner's books on meditation,[54] mindfulness can occur any time you are truly present. Sometimes even bird watching, eating slowly, or folding laundry can be meditation. Anything that gets you out of your head will do.

As the brain science behind meditation becomes more well-known, meditation and other mindfulness techniques are also becoming more mainstream. This has softened views about what really counts as meditation. Ancient rigors have given way to a growing appreciation for and tolerance of many more informal meditation practices.[55]

While we hope you will benefit from some of the time-honored methods below, you can practice being present in mini-meditation sessions any time that you would normally be waiting for something, such as in line at a store, while waiting for your computer to turn on, or even while riding in an elevator. You can turn these moments in which you might otherwise feel impatient into opportunities to focus on the breath and clear the mind. After all, being impatient will not make the moment pass any more quickly. Why not put this time to more productive (or unproductive, depending on how you look at it) use?

MEDITATION METHODS: DON'T GO DO SOMETHING, JUST SIT THERE[56]

Clearing the mind is not easy. Even the iconic yogi on the mountaintop notices the fly buzzing around his face or occasionally wonders how time can pass so slowly. Similarly, we can all benefit from meditation but many of us have difficulty clearing the mind. For that reason, it is easiest to start with guided meditation and move on to unguided meditation thereafter if you want more.

We suggest a few methods of guided meditation below, moving from easiest to more complex. Some of these techniques have been used by attorneys in the past with great success. We expose you to several tried and true methods for getting these powerful mind-clearing effects. Eventually, you'll be able to gain benefits from meditating for 20 seconds in an elevator, but this does not happen overnight.

Formal meditation practices can take hundreds of different forms. It doesn't matter which method you choose, as long as it works for you. No one is better than any another. The point of course is to relax the mind in order to counteract stress, give the mind a rest, and improve mental health and focus, which will in turn improve physical health. Pick a quiet place to practice these techniques and a time when you will not be interrupted.

EXERCISE 1: SIMPLE MINDFULNESS AWARENESS MEDITATION

One common form of meditation is to pick a short period of time to meditate, sit upright and erect, calm your mind as best you can, and begin focusing on your breath. As thoughts arise, acknowledge them, and just let them go, bringing your attention back to your breath. When you notice that your mind has drifted back to a thought, mentally label it "thinking" and come back to your breath.

EXERCISE 2: FOCUS ON A THUMBTACK

This is a technique you can use in the office. Martial arts experts ask students to focus on one point, in order to relax the mind, which they claim will round out an individual's entire life in remarkable ways. Martial arts teachers claim that not just you but your family and friends will notice an unbelievable difference in your overall well-being if you use this focus technique regularly.

The technique is simple. Put something, for example a red thumbtack, on the wall directly in front of where you sit and stare during the work day. Pick times throughout the day when you are feeling frazzled from multitasking to focus intently on the thumbtack. A less agitated mind is a more efficient mind, one that can complete tasks more quickly and more successfully than an agitated mind. I still use this technique and it works for me.

EXERCISE 3: BREATH COUNTING MEDITATION

Another very simple way to begin mediating is to sit quietly, slow the breath, and start counting your breaths, focusing only on the breath and the numbers. You can count from 1 to 10 a number of times, count from 1 to 50, count forward or backwards, or count in any other increment that feels right to you. Pick whatever approach helps you sit there for 10 to 15 minutes, increasing the time as you feel more comfortable.

Other counting methods are more involved but still pretty simple. In his book, *Mindfulness for Law Students*,[57] and in his first-year Jurisight program at Miami School of Law, Professor Scott Rodgers teaches the ancient 4–7–8 counting meditation to law students. Under this technique, you sit calmly in a quiet place and inhale for four counts, retain your breath at the top of the inhale for seven counts, then exhale for eight counts. Professor Rodgers teaches these future lawyers to accompany their breathing exercise with a hand gesture, starting with a loose fist, slowly opening the hand while inhaling, stretching the fingers out long while retaining the breath, then slowly closing the hand into another loose fist while exhaling. His students have found this exercise to be deeply calming and clarifying.

EXERCISE 4: MEDITATION ON AN OBJECT

This visual meditation technique is fantastic for focusing the mind. It is a powerful antidote to fragmented or incomplete observation, which frequently afflicts lawyers due to multitasking. This fragmentation also affects clients and witnesses in court hearings. Constant bombardment of our senses with stimuli overwhelms our senses' ability to pay complete attention to one object or event at a time, which impairs our ability to do our jobs optimally. This meditation not only focuses us, but also strengthens willpower. It is also fun because you can gain deep appreciation for the most mundane things.

Because we are conditioned to be to be task-driven, this task-oriented meditation is easier for beginners. It gives the mind something to focus on and tricks the mind into staying present. It doesn't matter what object you choose to focus on as long as it is small enough to scrutinize carefully without moving your head and large enough to see without squinting or straining your eyes. The candle glow above is one example, and this is a broader view of object meditation. In their Mindfulness and Professional Responsibly class at the University of Miami, Professors Scott Rogers and Jan Jacobowitz use a raisin, asking students to slowly examine the raisin, to see it, smell it, roll it, touch it, for several minutes.

To do the exercise, pick your object and a set a specific amount of time to meditate, say 3 to 5 minutes. Begin with a breath counting meditation to calm the mind. Once the mind is calm and present, open your eyes and begin to slowly study the object. Every time the mind strays, simply note that it has strayed and bring it back to the object. As you look at the object in detail, try to notice every detail without judgment. Notice how the light falls on the object. Does it induce any changes in its texture or color? Are there interesting shapes to observe? Is the surface rough or smooth? Try to simply observe without labeling what you see or judging it.

EXERCISE 5: BREATH WITH POSITIVE AND NEGATIVE MEDITATION

Taken from a school of Buddhism, this form of meditation is fantastic for neutralizing negative emotions. Sit and breathe in a positive attribute, then exhale its opposite. Start with these and move on with your own opposites:

> Breathe in white light, breathe out dark smoke.
> Breathe in kindness, breathe out cruelty.
> Breathe in courage, breathe out fear.
> Breathe in humility, breathe out pompousness.
> Breathe in beauty, breathe out ugliness.

Keep going with the opposites that apply most to your own current experiences.

EXERCISE 6: GUIDED IMAGERY

After a painful major surgery, we calmed my mother down and soothed her fears by using guided imagery of memories from her childhood. When one scene stopped working, we repeated the process by recalling other memories that we knew she cherished. Alternately, we imagined beach scenery or the smell of fresh cut grass. The technique relieved her anxiety. Perhaps more importantly, it calmed *us* down, reminding us of that infamous airplane directive about putting your own mask on first before assisting others.

To get started with guided imagery, remember a place where you had a fabulous memory. Close your eyes. See the place. Feel it, smell it. Imagine what you are doing there, running in a field, swimming in the creek, whatever you can remember about this fabulous place. Describe the place and these sensations in great detail, either aloud or in your mind. See Chapter 7, Exercise 17 to create your own personal inner retreat.

EXERCISE 7: YOGA NIDRA
MEDITATION WITH PROVEN MENTAL HEALTH BENEFITS

A recent study published in the *Indian Journal of Physiology* found that Yoga Nidra techniques reduced diabetes symptoms as well as the need for prescription drugs. It is also said that Gandhi practiced Yoga Nidra on trains between speaking engagements, and Swami Veda Bharati reportedly used it to learn a new language overnight.

Yoga Nidra is gaining popularity in the United States The Army Surgeon General and Defense Center of Excellence have endorsed Integrative Restoration® (iRest) Yoga Nidra, developed by Dr. Richard Miller, as a complementary and alternative medicine. The Department of Defense is successfully using it as a treatment for trauma and stress for soldiers returning from Iraq and Afghanistan, and its use by civilian stressed-out individuals is growing at business and community programs, hospitals and clinics, and universities across the country. Practitioners report that a 20–30 minute session of Yoga Nidra typically affords the effects of 3 to 4 hours of deep, restful sleep.

Yoga Nidra is best learned from a trained teacher (co-author Hallie Love is trained to teach Yoga Nidra). The basic practice involves lying down in a comfortable position or sitting in a chair, if that's more comfortable. You close your eyes and are guided through a variety of techniques including rotation of consciousness, body scanning, breath awareness, visualization, and the use of imagination while in a deep state of relaxation and meditation. You continue to feel the beneficial effects such as greater calm, clarity, equanimity, and positive emotions long after the session has ended. Practitioners also report improved sleep in general.

Here is a brief excerpt from a Yoga Nidra practice: Begin scanning your body while releasing all unnecessary tension in your forehead, eyes, tongue, jaw, shoulders, arms, torso, and legs. Bring attention to your senses. Allow them to be open and receptive, allowing perceptions to come to you. Direct your attention to outside sounds; distant sounds. Allow your sense of hearing to range into the distance.

Now gradually withdraw your senses back into this room. Develop your awareness of this room, its sounds, smells. Develop your awareness of your body, your mouth, nose, ears, and eyes and the sensation of air caressing your skin, the feeling of space around your body, the surface that is supporting your body, the heaviness or lightness of your body.

Become aware of sensations of any tensions and the feeling of letting them go; feeling yourself as receptive, each perception unfolding without thinking about what you're sensing. Simply allowing each sensation to arise naturally in your awareness just as it is. Concentrate on the flow of the breath between the navel and the throat. Feel the breath moving along this passage.

As you inhale, the air rises from the navel to the throat, as you exhale, it falls from the throat to the navel. And mentally counting down from seven to one while sensing the abdomen rising and releasing as the breath naturally flows in and out: seven inhaling abdomen rising and expanding; seven exhaling abdomen releasing and relaxing; six inhaling abdomen rising and expanding; six exhaling abdomen releasing and relaxing; five inhaling abdomen rising and expanding; five exhaling abdomen releasing and relaxing; four inhaling abdomen rising and expanding; four exhaling abdomen releasing and relaxing; and continuing on with your body's own natural breathing rhythm—alert, attentive, completely absorbed in counting. Long pause.

Let the counting fall away, and become attentive to the flows of relaxation throughout the body—in the mouth, ears, eyes, forehead, scalp, back of the neck, inside the throat, in the arms and hands, torso and pelvis, legs and feet, the body deeply relaxed. Long pause.

Once again become aware of your breathing, aware of your natural breath, aware of your breath through the nostrils. As you inhale, feel the life-giving force of the breath permeate your whole body. Take a long, slow, deep breath and become aware of your relaxed body and your physical existence, your surroundings, the surface you are laying on, the room you are in, and start making small movements transitioning to your natural state of being alert and awake, relaxed and recharged.

EXERCISE 8: MEDITATION ON A BRIEF

In his book about transforming the legal profession, *Transforming Practices*, Steven Keeva describes several forms of meditation, including an extremely valuable one he heard about from attorney Steven Schwartz called "meditating on a brief." Schwartz says he often spends the first 15 to 20 minutes of a morning meditation practice outlining briefs, oral arguments, and settlement orders, creating to-do lists, and considering other nagging work problems he has on his mind.[61] Schwartz engages in this work-related mind-clearing meditation before he engages in a more formal sitting practice.

While it does not necessarily work every time in the same way, Schwartz reaps incredible benefits from the "meditation of a brief" practice. Schwartz describes how this first, early morning time can be the most productive time of the day because the mind is not yet operating in a linear way. It free associates so one is not trapped by thinking about what comes next. Schwartz reports being able to come up with 90 percent of a document's first draft this way, in a fraction of the amount of time such a creative task might otherwise take. Those first moments of the day, when the mind is in the penumbra between waking and sleep are indeed the most insightful and precious.

DEEPENING YOUR PRACTICE

In concluding this chapter, we encourage you to learn more about meditation. Once you have tried some of the techniques we describe here, you may find that you want to go further by taking instructions from a regular meditation teacher, attending meditation classes, or even participating in overnight retreats. Some lawyers report that these overnight retreats create exponential growth in their meditation insights and the benefits they gain as a result. While there are many places around the country where attorneys can experience these retreats, some that have worked specifically with lawyers include Spirit Rock Meditation Center in Marin County, California, the Center for Contemplative Mind in Society in Massachusetts, and the Vallecitos Mountain Refuge in Northern New Mexico. ✳

9

Mindful Lawyering and Emotional Intelligence

Yoga heals the body, but as we've alluded to all along, it does much more for the mind. This is especially true when yoga poses are combined with some form of meditation. Given the many benefits, perhaps it is not surprising that yoga and meditation are growing exponentially in the United States. These techniques are also being used to heal bodies and minds in unusual settings here and abroad. For example, yoga has become a popular way for women to transform their lives in the West Bank. Yoga principles are being used to help homeless people in the United States, to help heal people in United States prisons, and to improve the tragic and disrupted lives of people in refugee camps throughout the world. As we saw in Chapter 8, Yoga Nidra (a form of meditation) is being used to heal U.S. soldiers returning from war. Yoga and meditation are also used in numerous hospitals around the country to aid in the healing process, both physically and mentally. These techniques are also being used to create a safe space in schools around the nation, where students face difficult and dangerous conditions every day.

If mindfulness practices like yoga and meditation can provide so much relief from suffering in so many settings, what role might they play in shaping the role of lawyers in society and even the law itself? This question is explored in this final chapter.

WHAT IS MINDFULNESS AND HOW CAN IT HELP ME?

Mindfulness includes yoga and meditation, the general topic of this book. It is a method of training yourself to see what arises in your own mind and body more clearly, so you can be more present, more grounded, and happier. It can also help you become more successful in meeting the challenges of practicing law.

Mindfulness is an intentional shift of awareness that can rewire neurological pathways to create long-term benefits in health and wellness. Mindfulness can not only improve your health as we've explained in the preceding chapters, but can also foster emotional intelligence so you react to difficult situations in ways that enhance your well-being and the well-being of others.

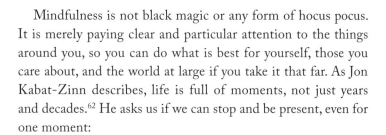

Mindfulness has been associated with the following traits:

Leadership skills

Attuned communications

Emotional balance

Fear modulation

Flexibility in response tactics

Empathy

Insight

Heightened sense of morality

Better interpersonal skills

Mindfulness is not black magic or any form of hocus pocus. It is merely paying clear and particular attention to the things around you, so you can do what is best for yourself, those you care about, and the world at large if you take it that far. As Jon Kabat-Zinn describes, life is full of moments, not just years and decades.[62] He asks us if we can stop and be present, even for one moment:

> A good way to stop all the doing is to shift into the "being mode" for a moment. Think of yourself as an eternal witness, as timeless. Just watch this moment, without trying to change it at all. What is happening? What do you feel? What do you see? What do you hear?[63]

ENGAGING IN A FULLER LIFE

Kabat-Zinn borrows a quote from Wu-Mein, saying "If your mind isn't clouded by unnecessary things; This is the best season of your life."[64] This brings us to mindfulness and happiness. While it may not be necessary to be happy in order to practice law well, it certainly makes life more fulfilling. In his book about the mindfulness program at Google, *Search Inside Yourself*, Chade-Meng Tan explains why it feels good to stop and experience the here and now:

> By letting go of grasping and aversion, we can fully adopt the letting-go mind and also fully experience life more vividly with the letting-go mind because it frees us from the noisy interference of grasping, aversion, and suffering.[65]

Studies of mindfulness and attorneys, a notoriously unhappy group, show that mindfulness meditation in legal practice can drastically improve attorney happiness, by creating perspective and balance.[66] Since mindfulness techniques like meditation or yoga allow one to focus on the present, calm the mind, and become deeply focused, they improve one's capacity to control emotions and improve one's life both inside and outside the law.[67] Yes, they can even make you happier.

ENGAGING IN BETTER LAWYERING

Naturally, present awareness can improve your ability to practice law, by putting your experiences in perspective in all areas of life. In *Mindfulness for Law Students*, Scott Rodgers claims that he believes he graduated first in his law school class because he is a long-term meditator and had learned to watch the storms and enjoy the show.[68]

We already have discussed numerous studies involving non-lawyer general populations, but studies of yoga, meditation, and the legal community show that mindfulness can help lawyers derive more career satisfaction and provide better and more efficient services to clients through better listening and negotiation skills.[69] Mindfulness can also reduce the number and severity of lawyer mistakes. Perhaps more obviously, yoga and meditation provide foundational tools to improve conflict resolution, foster ethical behavior, and avoid the negative emotions that sometimes get in the way of producing the best possible result for a client.

This comports with evidence from other fields. For example, in his mindfulness program at Google, Chade-Meng Tan was able to empirically show that mindfulness practices increase professional success, by improving emotional intelligence and interpersonal interactions. For example, investment advisors at American Express with mindfulness training made more money on average than those without the training.[70] Meng Tan explains that the main difference between good and great leaders is that great leaders have compassion for others that shows, and are deeply ambitious for the greater good, whether that is the good of the organization or some greater societal good.[71] In other words, those trained in mindfulness have the unique capacity to show both great ambition and personal humility, as well as a concern for something greater than their own advancement. These things cannot be faked but they can be learned, which is one of the primary lessons of *Search Inside Yourself*.

Similarly, in his book *Full Catastrophe Living*, Jon Kabat-Zinn describes his eight-week mindfulness-based stress reduction (MBSR) program at the University of Massachusetts Medical Center, through which very sick and suffering individuals have found great relief through mind-body connections like those described here.[72] The book tells amazing stories of transformation, and we highly recommend it. As Kabat-Zinn explains, bringing mindfulness to any activity can transform that activity into a form of meditation.

Mindfulness dramatically amplifies the probability that whatever activity in which you are engaged will result in expansion of your perspective and of your understanding of who you are. Much of the practice is simply remembering, reminding yourself to be fully awake—not lost in waking sleep or enshrouded in the veils of your thinking mind. Intentional practice is crucial to this process because the auto-pilot mode takes over so quickly when we forget to remember. As Kabat-Zinn explains:

> I like the words remember and remind because they imply connections that already exist but need to be acknowledged anew to remember, then, can be thought of as reconnecting with membership with the set to which what one already knows belongs. That which we have forgotten is still there, somewhere within us. It is access to it that is temporarily veiled. What has been forgotten needs to renew its membership in consciousness.[73]

To find the domain of being, we need to learn and practice mobilizing our powers of attention and awareness during exercise. By doing this, bringing mindfulness to any activity makes us better at that activity. As a result of these benefits, many professional organizations, including some law firms, have embraced meditation and yoga techniques with an eye toward improving productivity and employee health and wellness. These organizations have found that offering opportunities at work for yoga and meditation improves the performance and well-being of participants.[74]

Mindfulness training is also becoming a regular part of legal education, something you missed if you already graduated. Law professors are researching the effects of mindfulness on legal practice, and yoga and meditation are no longer fringe activities among lawyers and law professors. Yoga and meditation programs are now offered at 20 accredited law schools and some states include meditation in continuing legal education programs on professionalism and ethics.[75] In addition, over 25 law review articles have been written on the positive effects of yoga or meditation on the legal profession,[76] and Harvard Law School has featured several symposia on these topics in connection with the world-renowned Harvard Negotiation Project.[77] Additionally, a recent issue of the Journal of Legal Education contained a series of scholarly articles dedicated to the positive influences that stronger mind-body connections among lawyers might have on the profession.[78]

MINDFULNESS AND EMOTIONAL INTELLIGENCE

As Chade-Meng Tan explains throughout his book, *Search Inside Yourself*, emotional intelligence skills—knowing what others are thinking, responding to others in a way that promotes positive responses in situations, and being able to read people and groups—are perhaps the most critical skills for all professionals who deal with people regularly. While he leaves the door open to other possibilities, meditation and reflective journaling are the only methods he knows of for learning emotional intelligence.

Control of emotions is a huge part of emotional intelligence. While it is impossible to stop an emotion from occurring (it'll just bubble up somewhere else if you try), we do have the full power to welcome the emotion and then let it go, and perhaps with practice, to let it go immediately. Chade-Meng Tan describes this practice as comporting with the Buddhist metaphor of "writing on water."[79] Let the emotion come, but train yourself to let it go in the same way that writing on water would disappear.

Mindfulness can also help others around us. It gives us a unique glimpse at self-awareness and perhaps self-improvement. Unfortunately improving ourselves so we can serve others better is often painful because it requires finding and working with our own faults. One of those faults is often impatience, another a lack of humility, as this story from a large-firm attorney demonstrates:

Oh poor me, I thought as I entered the firm during a particularly awful period, in which we had lost a few lawyers, we had more work than ever, and there was a horrible political battle going on. Life really stunk. We had workplace yoga, attended mostly by staff, not attorneys, in the office. I entered yoga one day feeling really down and put upon. Why me? As I looked around, I saw the faces of the staff, who suffered the same horrible work conditions, but with very little pay, and also very little control over their day to day lives. I knew some had personal problems, others were having financial difficulties. In a conversation with the yoga instructor after the class, in which she explained that she was going through a painful break-up, I realized that my life was far better than most people's, and also realized how little humility I regularly bring to my everyday life. I am so important and put upon. Again, poor me. If I could bring one trait to lawyers, be it myself alone or all of us together, it would *not* be kindness, non-harming, or even truthfulness. Rather it would be humility. Most of us lack it in spades.

If you look around your own office, you will likely find similar things: people in power walking around like they own the place, rushed and hassled, put upon, ordering people around. The implication was that important people matter and their time is more valuable than that of unimportant people. This lack of humility is an impediment to being truly mindful in law practice and the practice of living. The lesson? We live lives of privilege, and we need to recognize this for our benefit and the benefit of others.

In summary, by controlling our stress, we can build better self-awareness which will unquestionably lead to a more successful career, not to mention personal life. This is because people who accurately assess their own strengths and weaknesses are more successful.[80] Genuine self-knowledge develops empathy, kindness, and better interpersonal skills. This news is both good and bad. It is very clear what you have to do and perhaps even how to do it. The bad part is that to do this, we need to let go of ego, stop thinking about how, cool, smart, and special we are, and start noticing these traits in others. We need to actually focus on others, which is a tall order indeed for most of us. In other words, we need to remember to practice humility whenever we can.

YOGA, MEDITATION, AND PROFESSIONALISM

Lawyers garner great power in society, power that can easily go astray. We can use our voices to do great good in the world, but can also do great harm. Lawyers' actions, even small ones, affect the profession and the world in profound ways. Both future and existing lawyers can benefit from these lessons, which can help them thrive in practice. As she explained:

As lawyers, we must learn not to fear or criticize passionate arguments. We must learn to listen actively and speak our mind, but without becoming verbally abusive or hurting others. In class, I expect that you will maintain your professionalism when your classmates are speaking. Please pause and think before you speak or act. Will your actions be viewed by a neutral observer as hostile, threatening, or offensive? Even in jest, words are powerful and can be interpreted many different ways.

If you have hurt someone else, it is a good habit for the practice of law and in life to learn to apologize. It is not an apology to say simply that you did not intend to offend. It is an apology to say you are sorry you hurt another person regardless of whether you intended to or not.

An important component of professionalism is also to step into the other's shoes, in a manner of speaking, and see their point of view, and also to be committed to further dialogue. As lawyers, on behalf of our clients we often have to engage in ongoing communication with individuals that we dis-agree with, and sometimes even intensely dislike. We do our clients and our profession a disservice when we fail to do this in a respectful manner.

Being professional embodies one of yoga's most cherished prin-ciples, that of non-harming. It is always worth reminding ourselves that our actions affect others and reflect on our professions. In that spirit, we offer one last meditation exercise geared specifically for lawyers seeking additional emotional intelligence.

THE LAWYER'S PRAYER OR REFLECTION MEDITATION

This prayer or reflection meditation can be used in a very spiritual way or simply to gain insight into your own actions, reactions, and future path. The idea is to pick a set amount of time to reflect on your own past actions and reactions, not with regret or self-loathing, but as an outsider looking in, much like when reflecting on an object. The point is to learn and to avoid making the same mistakes again and again in interpersonal relationships.

Begin by breathing slowly and deeply and focusing the mind for a few moments while letting the cares and stresses of the surrounding chaos begin to fade. Start with breath counting to calm the mind. After the mind is calm, allow it to wander and observe the thoughts as they arise. Begin thinking of past situations that left you feeling emotionally drained, angered, embarrassed, degraded, worried, or hurt. When you think of a particular moment in your mind, latch on to it and start breaking it apart. Don't use the exercise

to reignite past harmful emotions but rather to observe the past as an outsider.

Think about how the situation arose and what led to the feelings. Think of the words or actions that you or the other person said or did that made you or the other person feel badly. Then think about how you acted or reacted to those feelings. Don't let your mind just dismiss your actions as justified or appropriate but reach into your past self in that situation and understand the root of your action or response. Dig out the roots of the emotion. Once you have realized what happened and why the emotions arose, try to visually create alternative endings, things you could have done that may have made the situation better for you or others.

For example, imagine that a superior comes into your office and begins to raise his voice, using a condescending tone and maybe even profanity. You respond with either anger or by internalizing the words that the person was using and forming a pattern of self-loathing or self-con-descension. Imagine the other person being stressed or upset, just like you sometimes are. Now imagine yourself responding with a smooth calm tone and showing under-standing of what is being said without becoming angry or self-loathing. Finish the meditation with the same breath counting you began with.

As we all know but often forget, getting angry or hating oneself will never hurt the other person, it can only hurt you. If you respond with calm and understanding at least you will feel less stressed, angry, or upset. In the end a less stressed, happier you will show through in your family, work, and health and that is what prayer or reflection meditation is all about, taking just a few minutes of your day and allowing your mind to free itself of all the here and now while focusing on who you want to be and the path you want to take.

LAW AS A HEALING PROFESSION

More and more, law has become a business. If that is the way we view it, it is not likely to be sustaining. Law is a healing profession in a complex world and thinking about it in those terms *is* self-sustaining. Thinking that you are bringing good into the world and actually doing so will help you love your work more.

In his book about transforming the legal profession, *Transforming Practices*, Steven Keeva describes seven different forms of spiritually-informed kinds of law practice.[81] In Part II of the book, he describes how to create a balanced legal practice in which both the lawyer and the client are fortified.[82] In a section entitled "The Healing Practice," Keeva describes many instances in which just listening to the client and finding out the client's real needs and desires can achieve far more for the client than one might have dreamed. In one case that Keeva recounts, an attorney was part of a team hired to sell a trucking company. One of the members of the team refused to write the sale documents until he could meet the client. As it turned out, upon further discussion, the client didn't really want to sell the business at all. By getting to the truth, the attorney was able to keep the client from making a painful, life-changing decision.[83]

In another part of the book entitled "The Listening Practice," Keeva describes a technique called letting the client talk himself or herself out.[84] When one is unsure of a client's desires, one can just ask the client to keep talking and eventually, the real issue or problem will crystallize. Ultimately, Keeva believes that lawyers can be part of a whole web of healing professions that include medicine.[85] He uses many medical analogies to make this point. As he explains, lawyers used to be the ones to break up street fights. Now they are surrogate fighters. He goes on to say:

> Extending the war is not the answer. Building connections is. Moving toward healing in your law practice requires developing an integrative approach to lawyering, understanding the kinds of concepts that only recently were seen as soft and touchy-feely in the field of medicine no longer are. Research from many sources…shows that whatever connects is healing; whatever separates can be lethal.

> Once you have established healing as your goal, you can move clients in that direction in a number of ways. One very simple thing to keep in mind, though, is a lesson that the medical profession has only recently begun to learn…the mere presence of a physician tends to have a healing effect on sick patients. What if you were to take this into consideration in the moments before you meet a client? What if, realizing that your very presence can have either a salutary or a corrosive effect, you were to begin the interaction ready to use your best approximation of good bedside manner?[86]

Imagine how this approach might change the entire legal profession and also make our work a lot more enjoyable.

WHAT'S NEXT?

Eventually, if you continue your study in mindfulness, you will come to a fork in the road where your studies cause you to look at your work and your life through new eyes, to look at whether what you do each day is on balance something that is beneficial to the world, or in fact is neutral or detrimental. At this fork, you may choose to revisit the options you have in life, as doing things that help others generally brings more life satisfaction than money or status.[87]

By helping us focus on what is important to us and to the world in which we practice, mindfulness can advance social justice. Mindfulness in the law can help attorneys see the law as interconnected to the rest of society. Knowledge of this connectedness has the capacity to change every part of society. In the future, it is possible that more and more professionals will embrace mindfulness techniques to improve their practices and their lives. Over time, mindfulness may even transform legal practice and the world it serves. ✳

ENDNOTES

1. Jon Kabat-Zinn, Full Catastrophe Living xxxvii (1990).

2. *Id.* throughout.

3. Lisle Baker & Daniel P. Brown, *On Engagement: Learning To Pay Attention* (2014) (unpublished article, on file with author), *citing* Paul Hammerness, et al., Organize your Mind Organize your Life, Train Your Brain to Get More Done in Less Time xv–xvi (2012).

4. Leonard L. Riskin, *The Contemplative Lawyer: On the Potential Contributions of Mindfulness Meditation to Law Students, Lawyers, and their Clients*, 7 Harv. Negot. L. Rev. 1, 8–17 (2002); Martin Seligman et al., *Why Lawyers are Unhappy*, 23 Cardozo L. Rev. 33 (2001).

5. Kabat-Zinn, *supra* note 1, at 95.

6. *Id.* at 99.

7. Robert-Paul Juster et al., *Allostatic Load Biomarkers of Chronic Stress and Impact on Heath and Cognition*, 35 Neurosci. & Behav. Rev. 2, 2–16 (2010) (finding that chronic stress is a catalyst for accelerated aging).

8. Eduardo Dias-Ferreira et al., *Chronic Stress Causes Frontostriatal Reorganization and Affects Decision-Making*, 325 Sci. 621, 621 (2009) (finding that chronic stress makes one unaware of changes in the environment that should cause a change in behavior, impairing good decision-making).

9. Disciplinary opinions on alcoholism and drug use are too numerous to even cite, but there also are many opinions dealing with straight-up depression or an inability to properly deal with emotions. *See, e.g.*, In re Samuels, 257 N.Y.S.2d 373 (App. Div. 1965); *see also Mental or Emotional Disturbance as Defense or Mitigating Factor in Attorney Disciplinary Proceedings*, Am. J. Proof of Facts 46, 2D 563 (2013) (describing "burned out" syndrome and discussing at length what typically causes attorneys stress as well as the likely mental and physical ramifications).

10. Amit Kauts & Neelam Sharma, *Effect of Yoga on Academic Performance in Relation to Stress*, 2 Int'l. J. Yoga 39, 39–43 (2009).

11. Alison Wood Brooks & Maurice E. Schweitzer, *Anxiety, Advice and the Ability to Discern Feeling Anxious Motivates Individuals to Seek Advice*, 102 J. Personality & Soc. Psychol. 497, 497–512 (2011).

12. F. J. Tsai et al., *Occupational Stress and Burnout of Lawyers*, 51 J. Occup. Health 443, 443–50 (2009).

13. *The Effects of Stress*, AllPsychologyCareers.com http://www.allpsychologycareers.com/topics/effects-of-stress.html.

14. Robert M. Sapolsky, *Why Stress is Bad for your Brain*, 273 Science 273 (1996).

15. Yvonne Ellis et al., *The Effect of Multitasking on the Grade Performance of Business Students*, 8 Res. Higher Educ. J., (April 24, 2010), *available at* http://www.aabri.com /manuscripts/10498.pdf (finding that the exam scores of students who text in class are significantly lower than the exam scores of students who do not text in class).

16. *Depression, Stress Linked With Brain Shrinkage—Here's Why*, Huffington Post, (August 13, 2012), http://www.huffingtonpost.com/2012/08/13/depression-brain -stress-shrink-volume-mass_n_1773242.html.

17. S.J. Lupine et al., *Effects of Stress Throughout the Lifespan on the Brain, Behavior, and Cognition*, 10 Nature Reviews Neurosci. 434, 439 (describing the deleterious effects of stress on the brain, behavior and cognition), *citing* S.J. Lupien & B.S. McEwen, *The Acute Effects of Corticosteroids on Cognition: Integration of Animal and Human Model Studies*, 24 Brain Res. Rev. 1, 1–27 (1997). See also S.J. Lupien, et al., *Stress Hormones and Human Memory Function Across the Lifespan*, 30 Psychoneuroendocrinology 225, 225–42 (2005).

18. Brooks & Schweitzer, *supra* note 11.

19. Heleen A. Slagter et al., *Mental Training Affects Distribution of Limited Brain Resources*, 5 PLoS Biology 1228, 1228–35 (2007).

20. Peter Huang, *Authentic Happiness, Self-Knowledge and Legal Policy*, 9 Minn. J. L. Sci. & Tech. 755, 775 (2008).

21. Jeffrey M. Greeson, *Mindfulness Research Update: 2008*, 14 Contemp. Heath Prac. Rev. 10 (2009); William S. Blatt, *What's Special About Meditation? Contemplative Practice for American Lawyers*, 7 Harv. Negot. L. Rev. 125, 132–33 (2002) (meditation improves concentration and even supports greater life achievements); Riskin, *supra* note 4, at 46–53.

22. J.A. Brefczynski-Lewis et al., *Neural Correlates of Attentional Expertise in Long-Term Meditation Practitioners*, 104 Proc. of the Nat'l Acad. of Sci. 11483 (2007); Paul Grossman et al., *Mindfulness-Based Stress Reduction and Health Benefits: A Meta-Analysis*, 57 J. Psychosomatic Res. 35 (2004); Kirk Brown & Richard Ryan, *The Benefits of Being Present: Mindfulness and its Role in Psychological Well-Being*, 84 J. of Personality & Soc. Psych. 822 (2003).

23. Charles Halpern, *The Mindful Lawyer: Why Contemporary Lawyers are Practicing Meditation*, 61 J. Legal. Educ. 641 (2012); Sindya N. Bhanoo, *How Meditation May Change the Brain*, N.Y. Times (Jan. 28, 2011) http://well.blogs.nytimes.com/2011/01/28/how-meditation-may-change-the-brain/ (last visited on January 17, 2013); Britta K. Holsel et al., *Mindfulness Practice Leads to Increases in Regional Brain Gray Matter Density*, 191 Psychiatry Res. Neuroimaging 36 (2011) (finding that long-term practitioners of "mindfulness-based stress reduction" meditation showed increased gray matter in areas of the brain); Richard J. Davidson et al., *Alterations in Brain and Immune Function Produced by Mindfulness Meditation*, 65 J. Biobehavorial Med. Psychosom. Med. 564 (2003).

24. Scott Rogers & Jan Jacobowitz, Midfulness and Professional Responsibility 27 (2012).

25. *Id.*

26. Martin Seligman, *Why Are Lawyers So Unhappy?*, Lawyers With Depression (Nov. 16, 2012), http://www.lawyerswithdepression.com/articles why-are-lawyers-so-unhappy/.

27. Charles Halpern, Making Waves and Riding the Currents: Activism and the Practice of Wisdom 57 (2008).

28. Rick Hanson, Buddha's Brain (2009).

29. Chade-Meng Tan, Search Inside Yourself 167–68 (2012) (citations omitted).

30. *Id.* at 154.

31. *Id.* at 167–68.

32. *Id.* at 125–26.

33. *See* Katherine L. Narr et al., *Relationships Between IQ and Regional Cortical Gray Matter Thickness in Healthy Adults*, 17 Cerebral Cortex 2163, 2167 (2007); see also Sara W. Lazar et al., *Meditation Experience is Associated with Increased Cortical Thickness*, 16 NeuroReport 1893 (2005).

34. Teppo Sarkamo et al., *Music Listening Enhances Cognitive Recovery and Mood After Middle Cerebral Artery Stroke*, 131 Brain 866, 866–876 (2008).

35. D. Sutoo & K. Akiyama, *Music Improves Dopaminergic Neurotransmission: Demonstration Based on the Effect of Music on Blood Pressure Regulation*, 1016 Brain Research 255, 255–262 (2004).

36. William J. Broad, The Science of Yoga 9, 77–102 (2012).

37. Amy Weintraub, Yoga For Depression 56 (2004).

38. Broad, *supra* note 36, at 99–101.

39. *Id.* at 195–214.

40. *Id.* at 40–45.

41. *Id.* at 44.

42. Healthy Sleep, Sleep, Learning, and Memory, Division of Sleep Medicine Study, Harvard Medical School http://healthysleep.med.harvard.edu/healthy/matters/benefits-of-sleep/learning-memory (last visited on July 15, 2013).

43. "'Smoking certainly is a major cardiovascular risk factor and sitting can be equivalent in many cases,' explained Dr. David Coven, cardiologist with St. Luke's-Roosevelt Hospital Center in New York." *Sitting: Is It As Bad For You As Smoking?*, Red Orbit (January 22, 2014) http://www.redorbit.com/news/health/1113051913/smoking-and-sitting-all-day-equally-as-bad-012214/.

44. Kabat-Zinn, *supra* note 1, at 26.

45. Halpern, *supra* note 27, at 5.

46. *Id.*

47. Riskin, *supra* note 4, at 41.

48. *Id.*

49. *Id.* at 44.

50. Steven Keeva, Transforming Practices 43–76 (2d ed. 2009).

51. C.N. Alexander et al., *Transcendental Meditation, Mindfulness and Longevity: An Experimental Study with the Elderly*, 57 J. Personality & Soc. Psychol. 950–64 (1989).

52. Riskin, *supra* note 4, at 46.

53. Rogers & Jacobowitz, *supra* note 24, at 7–13.

54. Jon Kabat-Zinn, Mindfulness for Beginners 83–84 (2012); Jon Kabat-Zinn, Wherever You Go, There You Are 68–69 (2005).

55. Rogers & Jacobowitz, *supra* note 24, at 3.

56. This is a common yoga and meditation joke, which appears in many published works, including Kabat-Zinn, *supra* note 54, at 11.

57. Scott L. Rodgers, Mindfulness for Law Students 43 (2009).

58. Richard Miller, Yoga Nidra (2005).

59. Integrative Restorative Institute, http://www.irest.us (last visited Feb. 12, 2014).

60. Miller, *supra* note 58, at 7.

61. Keeva, *supra* note 50, at 45–46.

62. Kabat-Zinn, *supra* note 1, at 26.

63. Kabat-Zinn, *supra* note 54, at 11.

64. *Id.* at 16.

65. Tan, *supra* note 29, at 110.

66. Rodgers, *supra* note 57, at 2.

67. *Id.*

68. *Id.*

69. Riskin, *supra* note 4, at 46–48.

70. Tan, *supra* note 29, at 83.

71. *Id.* at 201.

72. Kabat-Zinn, *supra* note 1.

73. *Id.* at 94.

74. Rhonda Magee, *Educating Lawyers To Meditate*, 79 UMKC L. Rev. 535, 549 (2011). Currently General Mills, Apple, Target, Google, IBM, Reebok, Nike, Yahoo, Procter & Gamble, and Aetna are listed among the top companies who encourage and have established programs for their employees to engage in the practice of meditation. Additionally, law firms such as Burch, Porter, & Johnson of Tennessee, Hale & Dorr and Nutter, McClennen & Fish of Boston, Leonard, Street and Deinard of Minneapolis. *Contemplative Practices*, Cutting Edge Law, http://www.cuttingedgelaw.com/page/contemplative-practices (last visited Feb. 17, 2014). O'Melveny & Myers in Newport Beach, Calif., and Dickstein Shapiro in Washington, D.C. have all reported using yoga, meditation, or some type of contemplative practice. Debra Cassens Weiss, *Yoga Is Becoming the New Golf, In NYC and Some Law Firms*, ABA Journal (Feb. 17, 2011), http://www.abajournal.com/news/article/yoga_is_becoming_the_new_golf_in_nyc_and_some_law_firms/. Employees of these firms have expressed great satisfaction in these programs and have incorporated it into their daily routines. *Id.*

75. *See How to Learn the Law Without Losing Your Mind*, Idealawg (September 18, 2012, 7:47 PM) http://westallen.typepad.com/idealawg/yogi-lawyeryogattorney/. Of these, a number of ABA-accredited schools offer yoga or meditation classes to students for law school credit, including Berkeley, Buffalo, University of California-Davis, University of Connecticut, University of Florida, Golden Gate, University of Miami, University of Missouri at Springfield, CUNY, and University of San Francisco law schools. Leaders in bar associations have recognized the value of mindfulness, as reflected by Professor Scott Rogers' presentation on "Mindfulness, Neuroscience and the Effective Practice of Law" at the 2009 annual convention of the Florida Bar Association, for which attendees received CLE credit.

76. For a representative sampling, *see* Colin James, *Law Student Wellbeing: Benefits of Promoting Psychological Literacy and Self-Awareness Using Mindfulness, Strengths Theory*

and Emotional Intelligence, 61 J. Legal. Educ. 215 (2012); Richard Rueben, *Bringing Mindfulness into the Classroom: A Personal Journey*, 61 J. Legal. Educ. 674 (2012); David Zlotnick, *Integrating Mindfulness Theory and Practice into Trial Advocacy*, 61 J. Legal. Educ. 654 (2012).

77. *See Program on Negotiation at Harvard Law School*, Harvard Law School, http://www.pon.harvard.edu/events/making-waves-and-riding-the-currents-activism-and-the-practice-of-wisdom/?cid=74 (last visited on January 17, 2013).

78. *See* Zlotnick, *supra* note 76, at 654.

79. Tan, *supra* note 29, at 106.

80. *Id.*

81. Keeva, *supra* note 50, at 43–76.

82. Id. at 19–85.

83. *Id.* at 87–88.

84. *Id.* at 107.

85. *Id.* at 95.

86. *Id.* at 95–96.

87. Martin Seligman, Authentic Happiness 8–9 (2013).

Index